THINK ABOUT YOUR RESPONSE

J. W. CLARK

ARK MEDIA, LLC

Version 1.01

Trade Paperback ISBN: 978-1-7357593-4-0
Ebook ISBN: 978-1-7357593-5-7

CONTENTS

INTRODUCTION

These reflections were written during a tumultuous period in which the planet was navigating a global health pandemic that suddenly eliminated traditional social interactions. We turned to technology to allow us to work remotely, conduct online schooling, and even visit with doctors via telemedicine. People were scared, frustrated, angry, and even bored—a perfect storm stoked by the twenty-four-hour news cycle and fueled by social media.

The news was dominated by tragic stories of lives lost to a virus, families in financial ruin, and an increased focus on issues of social justice. We had new appreciation and gratitude for healthcare workers and teachers and did our best to support the local businesses that were struggling.

That all took place during the run-up to the presidential elections in the United States, and voters entrenched themselves in a progressively hostile environment. Friendships were forsaken and families divided, making it seem like the entire world had lost its mind. A world that has never been lonelier and more broken is crying out for leaders that can help navigate this gauntlet of social implosion. To be silent is to be seen as complicit, but to be vocal is to add to the cacophony. So then, what is the answer, and how should a Christian respond?

It may be hard to believe, but none of this is new. The issue of sin has been around for thousands of years, but the solution still stands atop Mount Calvary. The foot of the cross is where all divisions are revealed to be artificial. Regardless of whether you are reading this book near the time it was written or many years have passed, the perspective of heaven begins when we are willing to judge our own actions and attitude more zealously than we view those of others.

The goal of this devotional series is to get you to think. In this book, I reflect on how a Christian should respond to surrounding cultural pressures. How can faith be the answer for any problem in the world if you are not able to be at peace within yourself? If a Christian is militant with their everyday words, how can the answer be love?

In the pages that follow, I have tried to stay away from specific issues, not because I am trying to minimize them or because they don't need to be named, but because I believe the answer to the root problem is seen only through eyes that look upward. But that doesn't mean I won't be candid. Sometimes it's necessary to have a difficult and direct conversation.

It's not my intent to make any public statement meant for the masses—I just want to have a one-on-one conversation with you. I have been thinking about some things, and I'd like to share them.

I have selected various passages from Scripture that seem to illuminate how a believer should respond to the cultural pressures confronting any society. I have tried to include candid stories from my life that have helped me understand where I have fallen short of the life the Lord has called me to live.

My suggestion is to read one of these chapters per day, to allow them to percolate within your mind. Some ideas will resonate with your existing beliefs, while other concepts might push you to the edges of your emotions. Each reader has a different lens of personal life experience that affects how we interpret the world around us. My prayer is that the Lord will use these pages to provoke each reader in a unique way.

1

WORRY (MATT 6:25–34)

Imagine you're having a terrible day that starts the moment you get out of bed. Your shower is cold, the electricity goes out, and you have a stack of bills on the table. Now pretend you've just won fifty million dollars in the lottery. Suddenly, you lose track of your bad day and are filled with happiness. None of the problems you were facing seem so large anymore.

Throughout our lifetimes, we will each experience trials, but the anticipation of those events is often worse. Our imaginations are what keep us from swimming in the ocean, for fear of sharks, or from walking in the woods when the full moon is out. Anxiety is the fear of the unknown, which can bring paralysis. It's the moment just prior to the doctor sticking the needle in your arm that always brings more angst than the shot itself.

In Matthew chapter five, Jesus spoke to the crowds on a mountainside. He covered a lot of important topics such as generosity and prayer, as well as keeping your word and valuing life. But he also spent time talking about people's tendency to worry about what might happen.

> "No one can serve two masters. Either he will hate the one and love the other, or he will be devoted to the one and despise the other. You cannot serve both God and money."
>
> — Matt 6:24 NIV

This is why my example of winning the lottery is relevant. How many worries and anxieties in your life would fade from your mind if you were holding a winning lottery ticket? We see money as power despite the fact that nearly seventy percent of all lottery winners go bankrupt within five years.[1] *Oh, but that's because most people cannot handle money, but I would be different.* Ironically, the same thinking that convinced you to worry about your future is deceiving you that your solution is money.

Our treasure is in heaven. That's the only safe storage facility. Focusing on earthly problems or worldly solutions is a guaranteed recipe for tension.

"'Therefore, I tell you, do not be anxious about your life, what you will eat or what you will drink, nor about your body, what you will put on.... And which of you by being anxious can add a single hour to his span of life?'"[2]

Our bodies were designed to release hormones that allow us to react to danger. Adrenaline gives us rapid energy by raising our heart rate, increasing our blood pressure, and expanding our air passages.[3] This chemical reaction is real, and many thrill seekers put themselves into dangerous situations to achieve this endorphin stimulation. But our bodies were not meant to stay in that state of panic. It was meant only as a temporary means to avoid peril.

We live in the twenty-four-hour news cycle. We worship news. As if embracing intravenous feeding from a central line, we suck in a nonstop barrage of information designed to keep us in a state of fear. We justify our habit by claiming to be "informed" and look down on those who prefer to hide their heads in the sands of ignorance. The information we gorge upon is an artificial selection of what someone else has determined to be important. If we had the ability to ask the Lord what was going on, would the same subjects even come up in the conversation?

Every four years, the United States of America holds a presidential election. When the dust settles, half the country is feeling anxious and fearful about the future, while the other half feels that their problems have been solved. One half believes they just won the lottery, while the other half feels like they just went bankrupt. But anyone who places their hope in the politics of earthly kingdoms will find themselves on the sidelines of God's plan. Four years later, the political winds shift, and the triumphs of yesterday are replaced by fears about tomorrow. How many election cycles need to happen before believers realize they've been putting their hope in the wrong god?

Are you saying we shouldn't vote or take an active role in politics that affect our nation? Everyone looks at politics the same way, by asking, "How is this going to affect me?" Wasn't that the same issue that Jesus was dealing with on the mountainside? *How are we going to get food? What type of clothes and possessions will I be able to have?* If the Lord is able to feed the birds of the air and clothe the grass of the field, will He not do the same for you?[4] The real question you should be asking is whether you believe the Lord is your source of provision? Will he protect you? Will he provide for you? If the answer is yes, then why are you reacting to the news or election outcome as if your answer is no? As we will discuss in the upcoming days, that doesn't mean you are silent or uninformed, but your reaction to what you hear says a lot about your faith.

> "For the pagans run after all these things, and your heavenly Father knows that you need them. But seek first his kingdom and his righteousness, and all these things will be given to you as well."
>
> — Matt 6:32–33 NIV

In other words, the Lord would ask the citizens of America, "Are you an American Christian or a Christian American?" Those phrases sound similar but are starkly different. One word is the noun and the other the adjective. One defines who you are, while the other is simply an attribute. Which is the primary driver in your life?

The world is clamoring for your attention. The television stations and internet sites will not make money unless they can convince you to let them run your priorities. But all they have to offer is anxiety and fear. I can always tell when the media is running out of hype, when they start running stories of shark attacks on some distant shore. Telling you good news is simply not an option because that doesn't attract consumers or sell advertisements. But the Lord has some good news, and he wants you to share it. The shadow of the cross is large enough to reduce any fear.

The antidote for trepidation is to fall more deeply in love with the Lord. Focus your attention on his heavenly provision and not on earthly problems. Let the perspective of heaven overwhelm your mind.

Jesus doesn't need you to defend him. He wants you to follow him. Be a proud member of your nation and its election process, but remember you are a citizen of heaven. Be informed about the issues that affect your community, but be equally informed about the principles contained in Scripture. "'Therefore do not worry about tomorrow, for tomorrow will worry about itself. Each day has enough trouble of its own.'"[5]

2

EVERYONE NEEDS A CAUSE (ACTS 6–9)

A believer named Stephen was one of the first deacons appointed by the apostles. He was full of God's grace and even performed signs and miracles among the people.[1] At some point in time, he was involved in a disagreement with a group of people called the Synagogue of the Freedmen, who, ironically, took away Stephen's freedom. What started as a difference of opinion ended up in debate, and they couldn't stand up to his wisdom. As is often the case with debates, they lied and falsely accused him because when you worship your cause, lying and deception are acceptable strategies.

Stephen was brought before the Sanhedrin to answer the charges brought against him. In response, he gave an eloquent summary of the history of the Jews to demonstrate that it was not a new cause but one they all should have been pursuing. Stephen spoke the truth about their complicity in the death of Jesus and all the prophets that came before him, and the court turned against him. "They were furious and gnashed their teeth at him."[2] Stephen looked up and saw an open vision of heaven, with Jesus standing at the right hand of God. He was no longer interested in the debate. The time had come to give a testimony. He simply spoke what he saw, and that resulted in his execution. As Stephen's body was being crushed by rocks, his last words on earth were used to defend the very people that had killed him: "'Lord, do not hold this sin against them.'"[3]

Everyone needs a cause. It gives you energy and determination in the face of insurmountable odds. A clever coach can convince the members of their team that they are the underdog, the team no one believes is able to win. That trainer is trying to leverage the energy hidden within their players to take their game to the next level.

In the wake of World War I, the German people were languishing in their defeat. Their pride was severely wounded, and they needed a new cause. That state of mind proved to be fertile ground for the seeds of a very dangerous ideology. When Adolf Hitler began his rise to power in the early 1930s, he stoked the embers of national pride, giving the people a new campaign in which to believe. Hitler converted the youth organizations into feeder programs for his future army as he stole the hearts of the next generation of the German people. The painful lessons of World War II are numerous, but chief among them is the potency of the crusade. The passion of a generation can be harnessed in a powerful way, but history teaches us this can be very destructive. Everyone needs a cause.

Lots of fervent people in the world hold their opinions at dogmatic levels. Many of them have no problem with the destruction of those that disagree or don't share their devotion. This is exactly what happened in the case of a man named Saul. He was there when Stephen was dragged from his trial and sentenced by a violent mob in the backyard of the courthouse. Saul fully approved and volunteered to guard the belongings of those that were wholly focused on crushing Stephen's body with large rocks. Like many in our modern world, he didn't throw a stone but staunchly defended those who did. When your passion is comfortable with the destruction of others, it exposes the brokenness that has eroded your own foundation.

A great persecution broke out against the believers, and they were scattered throughout Judea, Samaria, and the ends of the earth. That shouldn't have been a surprise because what happened in Acts 8:1 was foretold in Acts 1:8. The symmetry of the references reminds us that the Lord is in control. In fact, during that time of persecution, the Gospel was spread to Ethiopia, which became one of the most vibrant areas of the early Christian church.[4]

But Saul was uttering murderous threats with every breath. The tremendous passion within his heart was unleashed on the early believers around Jerusalem as he went house to house, rounding up anyone with an opinion that differed from his own.

He was on his way to Damascus with letters from the high priest that allowed him to extradite any of the fugitives when, suddenly, he was knocked to the ground by a radiant light from heaven. "'Saul, Saul, why do you persecute me?'"[5] Paul responded in ignorance, for he did not know the Lord. He was about to realize he was on the wrong side of history.

> "I am Jesus, whom you are persecuting.... Now get up and go into the city, and you will be told what you must do."
>
> — Acts 9:7 NIV

Saul could no longer see. He lost his vision and was completely blind. He was led into Damascus and spent three days in total darkness before his physical eyesight was restored by a disciple named Ananias. "'This man is my chosen instrument to proclaim my name to the Gentiles and their kings and to the people of Israel.'"[6] When Saul's eyesight was restored, he had a fresh vision and a new cause.

Many movements in the world could be appropriate magnets for our attention, but the ends do not justify the means. We cannot sacrifice our faith on the altar of any ideology, but lethargy is an equal injustice. The solution is to focus on what the Lord is putting on your heart as he uniquely positions you to bring the Good News into the lives of a hurting world.

3

THE ENEMY OF MY ENEMY IS NOT MY FRIEND (MATT 26:14–27:10)

Jesus was reclining at the home of a man named Simon the Leper when Mary poured an entire bottle of expensive perfume on his head.[1] This was an extravagant act of gratitude by a woman whose life had been dramatically touched by the Lord. Jesus had raised her brother, Lazarus, from the dead, and she would be forever grateful.[2] We can also infer that Jesus had cured Simon of his leprosy by that point because of the fact that a party was gathered in his home. That was a time to celebrate, but some of those present viewed Mary's act as a waste of money and rebuked her for dereliction and a lack of stewardship. Among them was Judas Iscariot, who was using his position as treasurer to embezzle funds.[3]

Indignant over the missed financial opportunity, Judas went to the chief priests and offered to hand

Jesus over to them. They were delighted and agreed to pay him thirty pieces of silver. Judas had found a way to make up for the lost revenue from the perfume by temporarily aligning himself with the enemies of his teacher. He had plenty of time to reconsider his act of treason as he waited for the opportunity to betray the Son of God.

Several days later, they were celebrating the Passover and were again reclining at a table. Jesus knew of the impending betrayal and even warned Judas that his treachery would be one of the greatest mistakes in history. But for Judas, the ministry was about financial opportunity, and Jesus had lost track of the profit margins.

The rest of the group went to the Garden of Gethsemane while the traitor attended to his errand. While the Lord anguished in prayer, the deceiver led a group of armed soldiers to the secluded location. Betraying him with a kiss, Judas completed his duplicity, and the Teacher was led off in chains.

Filled with remorse over his actions, Judas tried to return the money and undo his disloyalty, but the chief priests absolved themselves of any wrongdoing and gave him no path to clear his guilty conscience. He threw the money into the temple and quite literally took the fall for the crime. His suicide sealed his role in history, and his name became synonymous with treason. Generations to follow would condemn him to hell, imagining him languishing in the depths of Dante's Inferno.[4]

The story of Judas Iscariot is a tragic tale. He didn't start out as a traitor—something changed along the way. Jesus had hundreds of followers, but he chose twelve to be part of his inner circle. During the three years of his active ministry, they would have gotten to know Jesus quite well. His compassion for the sick and his love for people would have melted any hardness in their hearts. So what brought Judas to the place where he became bitter enough to betray his role model?

The road of life is seldom straight. We can lose track of the worn path and end up in a place we did not intend to go. In that moment of realization, when reality defeats potential, the frustration of unfulfilled dreams can seduce you into ruinous decisions. Judas aligned himself with a cause that had ulterior motives and hidden agendas. We don't know what he thought the outcome of the arrest would be, but Scripture is clear that he didn't intend for it to end in death.[5] He ran back to the people in whom he had trusted, hoping to reverse the situation. He pleaded with them to release their prisoner and tried to appeal to their sense of mercy. But the wheels of corruption were already in motion, and they revealed whose side they were really on.

Judas let his personal frustration fester rather than dealing with the unhealthy passion in his heart.

He willingly overlooked the shadowy side of an organization he had embraced. He convinced himself that their cause had enough merit to prevent them from taking advantage of him. But the enemy of my enemy can never be my friend, and just because someone is going in the same direction as you doesn't mean you should get in their car.

We live in a world of polished marketing and targeted advertisements. Politicians spend lifetimes developing public personas designed to garnish votes. Organizations have large staffs focusing on the optics of each decision or statement they make. Not every goal is stated, and not every motive is revealed. Aligning yourself with anything other than the Gospel must be prayerfully and thoughtfully considered. Would you drink a beverage that had only one drop of poison? Would you congratulate a couple on their fiftieth wedding anniversary if they proclaimed they were ninety-nine percent faithful to one another? History is full of examples where convenient allies become future combatants. But our warfare is not of this world,[6] and the deceiver comes masquerading as an angel of light.[7]

Judas wasn't the only one to fail that night. Peter was also warned ahead of time but still denied his Lord three times. They both ran from the same scene and wept at the darkness in their hearts, but Peter allowed his guilt to lead him toward repentance.[8] Peter carried the weight of his unworthiness[9] for many days, but he didn't let it become the last chapter in his story. You aren't defined by any single decision, but you must be cautious to not allow your destiny to be sidetracked by any other pursuit that isn't fully aligned to the principles of the Gospel. Anything that is contrary to the message of the Lord must be called out and not overlooked. It's the little foxes that spoil the vine,[10] the small things that grow to become major problems.

Believers should be at the front of godly causes and the spokespeople for justice. We must be louder than our secular counterparts when it comes to topics that align with the message of the Gospel. We cannot be silent when our faith beckons us to speak up, but we must never align ourselves with anything that uses carnal strategies for achieving convenient outcomes. Jesus never needed to use the political machine of his day to achieve lasting change—this was accomplished by touching one heart at a time.

4

PASSION FOR THE WRONG CAUSE (JOHN 18:1–11)

The disciples had seen the signs and witnessed the miracles over three years of traveling throughout the world. Each of them had personally given up many things and pinned his future on the ministry. Many times, probably, they'd considered turning back and wondered if they had made the correct decision, but Peter was fully committed.

> "Lord, to whom shall we go? You have the words of eternal life."
>
> —John 6:68 NIV

Jesus's friends had warned him that going back to Jerusalem was dangerous, for the Jewish leaders were waiting to take his life.[1] They were fully committed to the journey, wherever it would take them. "'Let us also go, that we may die with him,'" they said.[2]

But not every disciple was in agreement on that fateful night when Jesus prayed in anguish in the Garden of Gethsemane. Judas Iscariot had heard enough and was cashing out his chips. For a payoff of thirty pieces of silver, he guided a detachment of soldiers to his Lord in an act of betrayal.

Imagine you were Peter, watching Jesus get arrested under the cover of darkness. Think about the three years of sacrifice and labor being squandered before your eyes. Everything you'd worked for, everything you'd dreamed–suddenly gone. You wouldn't give up that easily. You'd been carrying a sword for protection all those years, and the time had finally come to use it. After all, when Jesus was in the Temple, hadn't he violently overturned the tables of the money changers?[3] Righteous anger fills your mind because the time for action has come. "Zeal for your house consumes me," you think.[4] You're not like those other people, not like Judas. They are sellouts, compromisers. "'The kingdom of heaven has suffered violence, and the violent take it by force.'"[5] If you are being attacked, shouldn't you fight back? Shouldn't the Church be more intentional in confronting the cultural assault on Christian values?

Peter drew his weapon and tried to kill one of the

attackers, but he missed his intended target, cutting off the man's ear. Peter had enthusiasm—no one can deny that. But he had passion for the wrong cause.

Someone might think, *Wait a minute. Peter was trying to defend the Lord and his ministry on earth. How is that the wrong cause?* Yes, Peter had all the best intentions, but he let emotion cloud his judgement. Did the Lord need to be defended, especially in a violent way? "'Do you think I cannot appeal to my Father, and he will at once send me more than twelve legions of angels?'" Jesus asked.[6] The detachment of soldiers came armed with swords and clubs because that's how the world fights. What are the weapons you will use?

In today's increasingly polarized political and social climate, many feel their religious freedoms are under attack. They take to social media to defend the faith, often attacking those with differing agendas and opinions. They exert great fervor and take up the mantle.

On several occasions, I have glanced through the historical posts of my social media "friends" and have wondered if they were slipping into Peter's mistake. They have taken up the weapons of this world to defend where no defense is necessary.

> Jesus said, "Put your sword away! Shall I not drink the cup my Father has given me?"
>
> —John 18:11 NIV

Jesus strongly rebuked Peter for his physical aggression. The Kingdom of God was going to win the war, but not that way. The Lord touched the servant's ear and healed him.[7] People were not the problem, and violence was not the answer.

All four Gospels contain this story, but only John tells us that the servant's name was Malchus.[8] Many scholars have suggested his name was listed because he was known by the readers and had become a believer.[9] The theme of love pervades the Gospel of John because that's what changed his life. The man that Peter attacked had a name. He had a family and a life. Maybe he had children that would run toward his embrace whenever he returned home each night. What Peter's passion saw as the enemy, John recognized as a person, someone who also needed to know the love of God.

Passion drove Peter to commit assault and attempted murder, followed by repeated perjury in the courtyard of the high priest.[10] The downward spiral of bad decisions ended in bitter tears and brokenness. Everyone deserted Jesus and fled for their lives because human dedication is temporary and marked with convenience. Earthly zeal is grounded in selfishness and paved with good intentions. We cannot forget the Gospel in our attempt to defend it.

On the beach after the resurrection, Peter needed a reminder of where his allegiance should lie. *Do you love me? Then care for my people, don't attack them.*[11] Jesus repeated his question three times, the same number of times Peter had lied. You were created for motivation, but don't let it drive you to the wrong cause. God doesn't need strategic ideas that don't consider Scripture.

What are you passionate about? What drives and inspires you? As you reflect back on your life, do you see any casualties along the way? Are there people that became collateral damage as you confused them for your enemies? Maybe some names and faces are coming to your mind even now—relationships damaged for all the wrong reasons. Perhaps the time has come to put away the swords and mend some fences. Take some time to ask the Lord to hone your focus and use your energy for what he intended.

5

DISTRACTED PASSION (LUKE 10:38–42)

Hospitality in the eastern part of the world is taken very seriously. Travelers are to be cared for and protected. On one such occasion, Jesus and his disciples came to a village where a woman named Martha opened her home. As was the custom, she went about the necessary arrangements to feed the large group traveling with Jesus.

As the preparations were being made, Jesus talked to the family. When Mary, Martha's sister, heard his words, she lost track of the chores she would normally have been doing. She heard the voice of the Lord and forgot about all the other things competing for her attention.

When we open the door of our heart to the Lord, we are required to say no to the other things that contend for our allegiance. We cannot serve two masters.[1] In Martha's case, the culture of hospitality was preventing her from hearing the words of life. Yes, someone needed to prepare the meal, but an empty heart is worse than an unfilled stomach.

Martha is to be commended for opening her home and being generous. Many modern believers could learn a great deal by pausing on the opening sentences of this passage to consider whether they are being benevolent with the blessings they've received; helping those in need must be on the innate to-do list of every believer. Hospitality is central to many of the Biblical lessons[2] and finds expression in every modern society, but there comes a time when we must decide which culture will be our primary motivator. Will we prioritize the Kingdom of God over the kingdom of this world?

As Mary sat at the feet of Jesus and listened to what he said, we can almost imagine Martha gave her some unsubtle clues that she was needed in the kitchen, such as the banging of pots and sighs of disapproval. The world will try to get your attention on the priorities that it believes are important.

Lots of causes in the world are clamoring to be center stage. They see any attention given to another issue as competing for the focus of the world's singular conscience. If believers aren't careful, they will find themselves distracted like Martha, focused on the problem instead of the solution. We should be active in solving social problems because that was what Jesus did, but in order to be peacemakers, we must first hear the words of the Lord and let his instruction be the catalyst for our responses. Martha was distracted from what was most important. She was busy doing things, but not the *one* thing that really mattered.

Martha's frustrations boiled over, and she went straight to Jesus and asked him a timeless question: "'Lord, don't you care?'"[3] Believers have struggled with this question over the centuries, both in the privacy of the heart or spoken in the absence of listeners. With all the suffering in the world, you may feel like the Lord is ignoring the pain of your generation, but the solution is only heard by listening to the voice of God.

Martha felt like she was the only person doing the work that needed to get done. She was growing bitter toward her sister for not helping and resentful that she didn't have the same urgency for her cause. Is it okay that some people don't feel the same level of passion toward the things that stir your heart? Will it offend you if someone fights against an injustice different from the one you are focused on?

Years ago, I was a missionary living in Ireland and pastoring a small church. A man I'll call Connor attended our services, and he had been freed from a life of alcoholism by the message of the Gospel. He was excited about his new life and had a heart for his old friends still struggling with substance abuse, who tended to gather on the banks of the local river. He came to me and asked if the church could do something. I thought that was a great idea, but I knew I didn't possess the skills and life experience necessary to reach them effectively. The Lord had given me a passion for different types of needs, and I thought Connor was the perfect person to lead that new ministry.

When I approached him with the idea, he became irate. He viewed my proposition as a lack of energy and as an excuse to avoid helping people in need. He had no room in his mind for the concept that someone other than a pastor or priest should be leading such work. The more I talked to him, the worse his reaction became. Eventually, his list of my inadequacies grew to include things such as "You don't smile enough." He was compelled to share his opinions with a number of other people and eventually rallied a small group to split from the church.

Connor is not unique. There seems to be a growing belief that everyone in the world should share the same level of passion for a few selected causes, and "If you are not with us, then you are against us." But when we look at the myriad of challenges in the world, it becomes obvious that a divide-and-conquer strategy is necessary. We need people to lead in a variety of areas. That means that some people might support your cause but choose to be actively involved in endorsing another. Is that okay with you, or do you need everyone to be focused on the same thing?

Martha was passionate about hospitality in her home—nothing was wrong with that. Her mistake was insisting that her sister share her passion. Martha was trying to welcome the Lord but ended up alienating herself from his ministry. Overzealous passion can deceive us and subvert the very goals we intend. Mary was focused on Jesus and would end up being the one to pour the alabaster flask of expensive perfume on his feet as a preparation for his burial.[4] It was Mary, not Martha, who ended up showing the ultimate hospitality, and that was only possible because she had her priorities sorted.

Scripture says that Martha was distracted by her passion.

> "[Y]ou are worried and upset about many things, but few things are needed—or indeed only one. Mary has chosen what is better, and it will not be taken away from her."
>
> — Luke 10:41–42 NIV

Many needs in the world require strong leaders to rise to the challenge. "'The harvest is plentiful but the workers are few.'"[5] If we were to ask the Lord which of our passions should be the primary priority, he would likely answer that only one thing was most important. Maybe it's time that believers spend more time listening at his feet instead of criticizing the actions or omissions of others. Only when social activism is the second item on our to-do list can we have the clarity necessary to bring lasting change.

6

DON'T ASSUME GOD IS ON YOUR SIDE (JOSH 5:13–6:27)

Thirteen hundred years prior to the events of the New Testament, the Lord freed the nation of Israel from their bondage in Egypt and guided them into the promised land. Moses had led them for forty years, and Joshua had just brought them across the Jordan River. Many miracles had occurred along the way, including two mighty signs where the Lord altered the laws of physics and moved large bodies of water. The Israelites were told they would dislodge the people of the land of Canaan, and they were approaching the city of Jericho when Joshua saw a man standing with a sword drawn. Joshua needed some clarification and asked the man to identify which side he was on.[1]

The question seems simple on the surface, but it's actually quite complex. Was Joshua talking about the ensuing battle for Jericho, or was his inquiry broader? Did he even know the implications of what he was asking? He didn't have the full picture and brought his limited understanding to the discussion like excess baggage. He expected an answer that would fit into the worldview he'd created.

The question was actually backwards. The real issue was whether *they* were on the *Lord's* side, not whether he was on theirs. After forty years of rebellion in the desert, they were still focused in the wrong direction. Joshua and the people had no right to even ask the question after all that had transpired along their journey.

The first word in the man's response can be translated as "No." *I'm not going to directly answer the question you asked me because it's the wrong narrative.* The word could also be translated as "neither." *I'm not on either side—I'm on my side.* But Joshua was assuming the Lord would rally to support them. Why else would the Lord have commanded the Israelites to enter and conquer the land? Hadn't the Lord been on their side even before they left the bondage of Egypt? Clearly, the current occupants of the promised land were the enemies of the Lord's chosen people and their manifest destiny. To that the man basically replied, *Um, no. Some of your facts may be correct, but they have led you to the wrong perspective. Just no.* Before Joshua and the people went into their first battle, the Lord needed to correct Joshua's understanding. The man talking with

Joshua was the commander of the Lord's army. With sword drawn, the Lord is the one who commands the battle.

Joshua falls facedown in reverence and is told, "'Take your sandals off; you are standing on holy ground.'"[2] Does that sound familiar? In Exodus 3:5, Moses was given the same instruction when he met the Lord near a burning bush. Joshua had parted the Jordan River just as Moses had the Red Sea, and he was having another "Moses moment." Many scholars refer to this as a Christophany, an appearance of Christ prior to the New Testament.[3] Joshua was talking to the Lord himself.

Joshua was given specific instructions for taking the city. The people were to make a daily march around the perimeter in complete silence for a period of six days. On the seventh day, they were to parade seven times around the city and wait for the sound of trumpets. With a loud shout, they would see the walls of the stronghold come crashing down. All the while, the Ark of the Covenant was to lead them.

This set of instructions is oozing with symbolism. The number seven is mentioned in the Bible over seven hundred times. It carries the notion of completeness or perfection.[4] For instance, every seven years, the Israelites were to cancel debts.[5] There are seven phrases in the Lord's Prayer[6] and seven churches in the book of Revelation.[7] The people of God were led by seven priests who carried seven trumpets. Whenever they went forth, the tribe of Judah went out first,[8] which is significant because the name Judah means "praise."[9] In perfect completeness, the Lord would bring victory through worship, and the walls of the stronghold would collapse. The focus was to be on the Lord, not on the earthly challenges. Their perspective needed to be on him rather than on which group of people were their enemies. People are not your problem, and people are not your solution.

We all have challenges that we face, often on a daily basis. They can seem overwhelming and frustrating, especially if our lives are not going in the direction we hoped. The temptation is to place the blame on people rather than looking to the Lord for guidance. Will we become jealous if others find more success? Will we cling to the earthly battle or accept a heavenly realignment?

Maybe the Lord has appeared to you in ways of which you were not aware,[10] just as the Lord surprised Joshua on that day long ago. Perhaps he is trying to get your attention right now. Do you have time in your day for the possibility that he might need to correct your thinking? Is it time to focus on the solution rather than blaming other people for the problems? The Lord has specific plans for you.[11] He's not "on your side." The real question is actually whether you are on his.

7

FAKE NEWS (JOHN 8)

I had a friend ask me recently, "Did you hear the news?" With seven and a half billion people in the world, which story did they have in mind? Perhaps a famine or a drought was devastating millions of people in a distant nation. Were they going to talk about the grip of poverty or the lack of clean water? Or was the conversation drifting toward an overly vocal athlete or a morally adrift politician?

The role of the media has changed over the years. In the past, the news was reported by a handful of news agencies. That had two effects. First, nobody needed to compete for an audience because people eagerly consumed headlines from the handful of channels available. Second, if you wanted to influence what people learned, you only needed to control a few sources. A large donation or two might buy silence on certain world issues that were inconvenient to someone in power.

In the summer of 1994, I went on my first mission trip to Kenya. I was a college student on an eight-week adventure to some of the most remote parts of East Africa. On my very first morning in Nairobi, Kenya, disturbing developments were reported that would make my parents extremely nervous. The front-page story on every newspaper in America read, "Genocide in Rwanda." The people of America are not known for their geography skills, so every night, the evening news would show a chart of the region in conflict. My parents would gaze at that map with trepidation, knowing that their son was right in the middle of what would become known as the Rwandan Massacre.

A week later, I took a flight to the Democratic Republic of the Congo, which was known as Zaire at the time. The DRC shares a very large border with Rwanda, and I can vividly recall standing in a field, looking up, and seeing low-flying French F-16 fighter jets screaming over our heads on their way to the border. As I learned more about the situation, I was shocked to learn that the racial tension had been brewing for quite some time, and that was not the only humanitarian crisis in the region.

A few weeks later, I traveled to the largest United Nations relief operation in the world, located in northern Kenya along the Sudan border. The ethnic tensions in Sudan had been brewing for decades, but somehow I was completely unaware. How could stories like Rwanda and Sudan be unknown to a college student in the West? Why wasn't the news reporting on these tragic stories? With all the tales that were being told, why were these being avoided?

The internet has changed the way the world consumes news. Millions of sources of information exist, each presenting a different set of "facts." People are overloaded with information and calloused by the severity of the problems. As a result, stories must be marketed, becoming increasingly alarmist and stoking the fires of emotion. Jesus never had to deal with the internet while he was on earth, but he did need to address people repeating fake news.

In John chapter eight, a group of religious leaders dragged before Jesus a woman who had been caught in the act of adultery. The Law was clear on this topic and required the sentence of death by stoning.[1] But this inquisition was designed to be a trap. Would the Healer condemn her and uphold the Law or would he continue to show compassion? Jesus presented an existential threat to the social and political system, and he needed to be controlled.

The religious leaders presented irrefutable facts

and demanded that he address their narrative. But Jesus disregarded their version of the events and bent over and wrote in the sand. They persisted in a nonstop barrage of condemnation, and he continued to ignore them.

Their report contained gaps. Where was the man? If she had been caught in an act of sexual sin, then by definition, a man who wasn't on trial had also been present. Had she been set up? Was the testimony even true? Jesus didn't bring up these obvious holes because the situation didn't even justify a response. It was the wrong story.

Jesus understood the Law and the intent behind it. The Law reveals the need for a savior. The Messiah wasn't on earth to remove the Law—he was there to fulfill it.[2] Jesus stood up and cross-examined the witnesses.

> "Let him who is without sin among you be the first to throw a stone at her."
>
> —John 8:7 AMP

When the people heard this response, they walked away. They realized they had been focused on the wrong set of facts.

Fake news comes in two flavors—either lies about what really happened, or the deliberate presentation of a partial set of details. We can't be sure which type was being employed on that day in Jerusalem, but Jesus clearly had a totally different narrative.

When everyone was gone, he stood up and asked the woman, "'Has no one condemned you? Neither do I condemn you.'"[3] In other words, forget about the mistakes of the past and focus on making the correct decisions going forward.

We are being bombarded with emotional scripts every day, but you were never meant to carry the burdens of the entire world—that was the cross that Jesus bore. We each face a daily choice of whether to believe the coverage we hear. That doesn't mean we dismiss the facts that are difficult or that violate our worldviews. It means we must filter the information through the lens of Christ. *Is what I am hearing building people up or tearing them down? Is the information designed to build influence and political power, or does it soften my heart toward helping to meet the needs that are being presented?*

As you reflect on the episode of the woman caught in adultery, take a moment to consider where you fit in. Can you relate to the woman whose world was crashing under the weight of bad decisions? Are you a bit like the accusers, focusing on the judgement of others rather than compassion? Maybe the Lord is calling you to be a bit more like Jesus. The world needs to hear a different set of news, one of reconciliation undergirded with love.

As you go about the rest of your day, you have a choice about which set of details you will focus on. Only you can decide which story you will tell.

Are you enjoying this book?

Would you be willing to take a moment and leave a rating or a review?

This is the perfect way to let the author know that these words are impacting your life. Many potential readers wait to read books until they have received hundreds of reviews. If you believe that this book could impact someone else's life, please take a moment *right now* to leave a review.

–J. W. Clark

8

ARMED FOR BATTLE (EPH 6:10–20)

Have you noticed that everyone seems angry? I never thought I would miss the days of social media being filled with pictures of puppies and descriptions of what people had eaten for lunch. Regardless of political affiliation, blaming other people for the problems in society seems to be the full-time job of too many people. Offense is everywhere, and fuses are short.

At the time of the American Civil War, two families were living in Appalachia, the Hatfields of West Virginia and the McCoy family of eastern Kentucky. Both families largely fought for the Confederacy except for Asa McCoy, who joined the Union Army. That was the borderland, and the war was quite literally brother against brother. When Asa McCoy returned from the war, he was murdered by Confederate sympathizers, and suspicions turned toward one of the Hatfields. A series of disagreements over the ensuing years escalated to a breaking point on New Year's Day of 1888, when a group of Hatfields surrounded a McCoy cabin and attacked the sleeping family, killing two children, beating the wife, and setting fire to the home.[1]

Two days later, a posse of McCoys set out and captured several members of their nemesis. Additional raids killed three more, and revenge was at fever pitch. On January 19, 1888, large numbers of both families had an armed confrontation in what would come to be called the Battle of Grapevine Creek. After many casualties on both sides, twenty members of the Hatfield clan were apprehended and indicted. The Supreme Court of the United States got involved and ruled that trials would be allowed in Kentucky for the New Year's massacre. Eight of the men were given life sentences, but one was given the death penalty when he mistakenly thought confessing his guilt would result in leniency. But as they said, somebody had to hang—even in a state where the death penalty was illegal. In the moments before his execution, the accused man said, "The Hatfields made me do it." One hundred fifteen years later, the two families finally declared a truce.[2]

This story serves as a stern warning about what can happen when people take aggressive actions that they feel are justified by the behavior of others. Very likely, both families felt like victims, and both felt they were justified in taking revenge. I wonder how different history would have been if someone in either family had taken to heart the words of Ephesians 6:12: "For we are not fighting against flesh-and-blood enemies, but against evil rulers and authorities of the unseen world" (NLT). In other words, people are not your enemy.

The book of Ephesians ends with Paul encouraging us to put on the full armor of God so that we can make our stand in the world in which we live. He knew firsthand what being victimized felt like. He was beaten, stoned, and imprisoned.[3] But his strength was in the Lord, not his own ability to weather the trials of life. The armor of God prepares us for spiritual battle, but most armor is not intended for attacking.

The first armament in Paul's list was the belt of truth. That foundational equipment was designed to hold a sword, scabbard, or similar handheld weapon, without which the soldier would be defenseless on the field of battle.

The soldier would also need to have proper footwear to traverse the battlefield safely, and the breastplate was worn to protect the vital organs. Paul reminds us that our feet need to be fitted with the gospel of peace and that our journeys may bring us into situations that threaten to harm us. So it's fitting that the breastplate of righteousness would protect the heart of the spiritual warrior.

The shield of faith reminds us that we will be targeted by flaming arrows, while the helmet of salvation protects our minds. The sword of the Spirit is the only thing we possess that is meant for aggression, but the battle we fight is not an earthly conflict. We are waging war for the souls of humankind. Scripture contains the antidote for the poison in the world, and believers are called to administer it to those in need. It's the vaccine against the virus that spreads among us, the truth that has the power to demolish strongholds of thought.

But it's within our earthly nature to seek revenge on those that harm us or keep us from our freedom. We see it clearly in the modern political theater, where those on opposing sides of the aisle wage battles for votes and government control, pointing the finger of blame in every direction except toward themselves. But when you throw mud at someone, you not only get dirty, but you lose a lot of ground.[4]

The key to inner peace is understanding that people are not your problem. You might be tempted to think poorly about your boss or a coworker, or maybe you believe all your problems come from your spouse or a family member. *If only those politicians would stop doing what they are doing and start doing what I want them to do!* Or perhaps you are in a conflict with your neighbor or certain members of your community.

In the corporate world, conflict can arise that

may seem like a personal attack. I can remember one occasion that was particularly harsh and very personal. I wanted to "set the record straight" and fire off a scalding email, but instead of sending what I'd written, I deleted it. When I asked the Lord for insight, I began to consider what was going on in the other person's life that might have caused them to react in the way they had. Instead of returning the anger, I contacted the individual and asked if everything was okay. My simple action disarmed the confrontation and allowed room for the Lord to move. As they began to literally pour out their heart and emotion, I realized I'd won a spiritual battle by avoiding an earthly one.

You are an example to those around you. Will you use your voice to add to the noise and chaos, or will you be the voice of calm? Will you put on the full armor of God and fight the spiritual battle, or will you allow yourself to contribute to earthly conflicts?

9

HATE FOR THOSE WHO HATE (LUKE 9:51–56)

> Jesus resolutely set out for Jerusalem.
>
> — Luke 9:51 NIV

He was determined as he set his face toward the city that would become the stage for the ultimate sacrifice. He was to die upon a cross for the sins of the world, and that included the people in Samaria, which lay between Judea and Jerusalem. When the citizens of Samaria realized where he was going, they did not welcome him in their villages, which infuriated the disciples.

The Samaritans were the descendants of the people who broke away from the rest of Israel during the time of the Assyrian invasion.[1] Their history has been debated, but one thing is clear: in the time of Jesus, a deep-seated animosity existed between them and the Jews. Both groups believed their own traditions pointed to the location of the one true place of worship, so Jesus heading toward Jerusalem was seen as a political statement.

The disciples had become accustomed to Jesus traveling through Samaria despite their personal bias, but when the Samaritans openly shunned their mission, James and John were incensed. "'Lord, do you want us to call down fire from heaven to destroy them?'" they asked.[2] After all the time they'd spent with Jesus, this is what they'd learned? John is known as the disciple of love, yet he and his brother wished destruction upon an entire people group.

Is it okay to hate those who hate you? The disciples had peacefully traveled through the region without incident on many occasions, but their inner prejudice was revealed when they confronted the intolerance of the Samaritans. Imagine for a moment what they might have been thinking: *We're not the aggressors. We're merely returning the negative energy of a hate group. After all, shouldn't we eliminate all forms of hate, regardless of how it must be done? Sometimes, you have to fight fire with fire—to do whatever it takes. The end justifies the means.* Was this the mental justification that allowed James and John to wish harm upon people with whom they disagreed?

When I was an undergraduate student, I enrolled in an English course that often had lively classroom discussions. On one occasion, the instructor was reminding us that we had no right to insist that other people embrace our worldviews. We couldn't tell anyone that they were wrong. Truth was relative, and the university was full of progressive thought. Being an engineering student surrounded by classes in logic, I decided to test the professor's pronouncement. I made a dogmatic statement to which I knew the entire class would object. They reacted as I anticipated, demanding I retract my words. But I replied simply: "I thought you said we weren't allowed to tell someone that their opinions were wrong. How, then, can you object to what I just said? You're breaking your own rules." The class didn't know how to react, and the teacher had no response. She was staring into the mirror of her own intolerance. Luckily, no one in the class called down fire upon me that day.

None of us should tolerate hate, but the way we treat those with whom we disagree will determine the level of our own hypocrisy. Is it okay to hate those who hate, or does that just perpetuate the cycle?

Boycotts and strikes have always been effective tools of leverage against oppressive power structures. The rise of the unions in the early nineteen hundreds, for example, exposed the plight of the factory workers and coal miners of the industrial revolution.[3] But if we are not careful, the roles trade places, and the victims become the oppressors.

In modern times, some of these same strategies have been applied to groups and organizations on opposite sides of the political aisle. A restaurant is banned from a city for the conservative views of its owner, while a clothing company is shunned for its support of a specific liberal cause. Cries for tolerance are coming from both ends of the political spectrum, but only for ideas that they support. People claim to be sick of the partisanship but only offer more polarizing solutions as the answer.

If a restaurant refuses to serve a politician from a political party they despise, is that free speech or intolerance? When the name and home address of a mayor are posted online and an angry crowd gathers outside their door, is that social activism or mob violence? If fear is the motivation for social change, have we championed equity or simply swapped power structures? The answers to these questions are largely determined by whether you support the cause that is using the strategy. Jesus challenged his followers to be different.

"You have heard that it was said, 'Eye for eye, and tooth for tooth.' But I tell you, do not

> resist an evil person. If anyone slaps you on the right cheek, turn to them the other cheek also. And if anyone wants to sue you and take your shirt, hand over your coat as well. If anyone forces you to go one mile, go with them two miles. Give to the one who asks you, and do not turn away from the one who wants to borrow from you."
>
> — Matt 5:38–42 NIV

Jesus painted a clear and precise picture of the proper response to those we might view as our enemies. Ours can never be a message of hate or anger despite what other people do. If someone harms us physically, takes our possessions, or misuses our time—we are called to never use those same strategies in response. We must be examples of how to act and not reciprocate the destructive methods we observe.

Jesus wasn't afraid to rebuke his disciples when they were using the ways of the world to try to accomplish the goals of the Kingdom. They were confused, and they were wrong. When the Samaritans put a political spin on his ministry, Jesus refused to play the politician. He would not hate those who hate, and he openly rebuked his disciples when they did so.

None of us like being hated, and we all want justice when we are the victim. But are there ways that you have been on the wrong side of the equation? If I were to read your social media feed, would I see love or animosity? When you read or watch the news, what tactics and strategies are being fed into your mind? When you encounter opinions that stir your emotions, what type of passion comes out of your mouth? You are intended to love people, regardless of whether you agree with the ideas they espouse.

10

RESPOND, DON'T REACT (ACTS 15:36–16:24)

Paul the Apostle had a vision that drew him into the region of Macedonia. He was fresh off a major disagreement with his mentor, Barnabas, that caused them to part company. Taking Silas and Timothy, he traveled to Philippi, the leading city of that region, where he found a group of women that had gathered at the edge of the river to pray.

One day, they were followed to the riverside by a slave girl who had generated great sums of money for her owners by predicting the future. She began shouting, "'These men are the servants of the Most High God, who proclaim to you the way of salvation.'"[1] She kept this up for many days before anyone made an attempt to stop her.

Some people might wonder what harm was being done if her words were promoting the Gospel message. In fact, many modern-day preachers might have embraced her promotion of their ministry. Some might have tried to immediately silence her while others would have avoided confrontation at any cost. Paul waited for the right moment to turn and verbally rebuke the false spirit, saying,

---

> "In the name of Jesus Christ I command you to come out of her!" At that moment the spirit left her.
>
> — ACTS 16:18 NIV

Only two possibilities can explain Paul's actions. He either knew the girl was possessed by a spirit and chose not to address it, or he didn't understand her situation for several days. In either case, Paul chose not to react in the moment but waited to make a proper response.

There is a huge difference between a reaction and a response. A reaction is something that comes out of you, a backlash to being provoked. It occurs without the inconvenience of thought and often evokes regret. We can get caught up in the moment and neglect thinking about the downstream impacts of our actions. A response, on the other hand, is something we choose after weighing the various options. We consider the repercussions and calculate the cost of our actions or silence.

No shortage of divisive issues exists in the world today. One car ride during the traffic of the morning commute leaves no doubt that anger is only lightly veiled beneath the surface. A frustrated person can often be easily provoked into a social media rant that wounds friends and alienates families.

When it comes to lessons in restraint, the internet provides the perfect classroom. Scrolling past pictures of endless selfies and pictures of food, you pass a politically motivated post from a former schoolmate. You disagree with the stated opinions and roll your eyes at what you consider to be misinformation. Do you type a reply? Do you engage in an argument? Can you sleep at night while knowing that someone posted something in cyberspace that was incorrect? Maybe you unfriend them or cancel the friendship altogether.

My observation has been that people with peaceful lives do not complain or react without thought. If you are confident in who you are, then you really have no reason to correct your friends. But when the internal pressure of life flows too close to the surface, people react out of the pain of their own life experiences. When the questions of life run out of answers, we lash out at any injustice that our minds perceive.

Why is it so important for people to correct the

opinions with which they disagree? When life takes a turn in a bad direction, we look for someone else to blame. Politicians sell the belief that electing them will solve all your problems caused by their opponent. They need your vote and throw fuel on any fire that helps them ascend to office. But no recount of ballots will change who is on the throne. Referendums are for earthly rulers, but the believer's eyes must look to the true source of life. Having this type of perspective allows us to discern between moments that necessitate action and those when silence is the better choice.

Paul and Silas ended up in prison for ruining the neighborhood fortune-telling economy. The local politicians ignored the bondage of a young girl and the prison in which she'd been living. But Paul and Silas chose to sing hymns of praise rather than complain about their circumstances. When the Lord miraculously opened the jail cells, they had no reason to run for the exit because they were already free. They did not react to the incarceration *or* the open prison doors because neither event changed where they placed their hope. Their response brought about the salvation of the jailer and ended the cycle of reactions.

But even Paul didn't always make the correct choice. As he left Philippi for the city of Thessalonica as a free man, I wonder if he thought about his heated disagreement with Barnabas over a man named John Mark, who'd deserted the ministry years earlier. That defector would go on to be known simply as Mark and author the Gospel that bears his name. Barnabas responded to the desertion by wanting to give him a second chance, but Paul reacted much differently.

About forty years later, Paul reflected on his behavior as he was nearing the end of his life. Writing to Timothy, he expressed a change of heart. "'Get Mark and bring him with you, because he is helpful to me in my ministry.'"[2]

We don't know much of what happened to Barnabas, though tradition holds that he was martyred in Cyprus and buried by Mark.[3] No evidence shows that Paul and Barnabas ever repaired their relationship, fractured by the conflicting passions of the two men. Did Paul ever regret his choice and respond by reaching out to his old friend? Was it worth the division between two of the great members of the early church?

These three examples remind us of the importance of discernment: a fortune-telling girl by the river, the ensuing unlawful imprisonment, and a difference of opinion over whether Mark deserved a second chance. The situations in your life will differ, but the lesson remains the same.

The modern world needs believers that pray before they respond, people who choose to think before they speak. Whether on social media or in your daily interactions, will you see people as more important than debates? Is being a friend more valuable than being correct? As you are reading these words, maybe someone is coming to your mind that is no longer in your life because of a careless word. Make today your Barnabas moment and begin to respond differently.

11

GOD CARES ABOUT THE LITTLE THINGS (JOHN 2:1–11)

Reading or watching the news is dangerous. After only a few minutes, you can become overwhelmed by the sheer scale of the problems in the world. If you're anything like me, you read the news in small doses then try to retreat to a quiet place of peace. But some of the issues that society faces are deeply troubling and need to be fixed. We need every prayer we can muster.

Many problems never make the evening news. Things that don't involve famous people or violate the dominant narrative tend to remain unknown and obscure. These are the everyday issues that many of us face. A child who is rebelling against their parents or a marriage that is falling apart are equally important to those involved. What about the family facing a health challenge or financial trouble from the loss of employment? Does the Lord have time for ordinary issues of everyday people?

In every corporation or government, issues need to be prioritized and delegated. Large things get handled first and by the top leaders, while smaller things are passed down to subordinates. But that isn't how the Kingdom of God works. The Lord has the ability to multitask and can answer prayers about the "little things in life" even when the world seems to be overwhelmed with challenges.

In John chapter two, Jesus and his disciples are invited to a wedding in the town of Cana in Galilee. That was a familiar location for him and a spot to which he would return. His family was also invited, and we learn that his mother had a vested interest in the supplies, for Mary was the one who turned to Jesus when the wine ran out.

Weddings are supposed to be about the celebration of a union, but even modern weddings can be a tremendous source of stress for those that plan them. Everything is supposed to be perfect, with nothing going wrong. Wedding fails are a fun diversion on YouTube, but they can be heartbreaking if you are the one in the video. As time goes by, we can all laugh at what used to seem like a "big deal," but in the moment, even the small events are important to us.

> Jesus replied to his mother, "What does this have to do with me? My hour has not yet come."
>
> —John 2:4 ESV

Jesus was about to start his earthly ministry, in which he would preach to hostile congregations. He would confront religious leaders and threaten the political balance of power. Crippled and dying people would pursue him in desperation while even his own friends would plot against him. A lot must have been on Jesus's mind, yet he took the time to meet a need. It was a small thing, considering all that was to take place, but it mattered to the bride and groom. It mattered to his mother. Thus, it mattered to Jesus.

We learn in Luke chapter twenty that marriage doesn't exist in heaven,[1] but Jesus performed his first miracle at a wedding. To further stretch our modern minds, Jesus produced an alcoholic beverage for the guests to consume, and apparently one of very good quality! Many Christians want to overlook these facts because they make us uncomfortable—that's just not how we would have done it.

Jesus got involved in the everyday lives of people. He instructed that six stone jars be filled to the brim with water and a sample be brought to the master of the banquet. He met the need in overwhelming quality and quantity. Even in lesser things, he will do more than we can ask or even imagine.[2] When we give him our lives, his abundance overflows, "'a good measure, pressed down, shaken together, and running over.'"[3]

It's interesting to note that six jars were there that day. The number six can symbolize imperfection.[4] Jesus was meeting the immediate concern, but a much deeper need would be addressed on the cross. Wine was present on that day, too, but Jesus did not partake until his task was finished.[5] Life might not be perfect, but even the mundane has a place in his heart.

The story of Cana is recorded only in the Gospel of John by the disciple who had the closest earthly relationship with Jesus.[6] It was also the last Gospel written, by a man in exile.[7] As John looked back over his life and experiences with his Lord, he remembered that it had all started with a small issue at a hometown wedding, when Jesus showed that he cared about seemingly unimportant aspects of life.

Like the child of a CEO who knows they can interrupt their parent at any time—simply because they have that relational access—"Let us then with confidence draw near to the throne of grace, that we may receive mercy and find grace to help in time of need."[8]

The Lord hears your prayers. He wants you to be mindful of the state of the world he created, but he also wants you to know he is concerned about you. He has time for the minor things that loom large in your heart. Tell him how you feel and what is occupying your thoughts, then, as Mary said on that day in Cana when she considered the matter settled, "'Do whatever he tells you.'"[9]

12

IT MAY LOOK LIKE I'M SURROUNDED - (2 KGS 6:8–23)

Of all the things that seem to be lacking in the world today, perspective has to be near the top of the list. I've had the opportunity to visit many nations during my lifetime, and that has forever changed the way I look at the world.

I remember one trip to Tanzania in 2001, during which I was invited to dinner at the home of a local businessperson. The house was a distance from the city, down rain-soaked mud roads and deep in the forest. We were served baked chicken at a small table with limited seating. As a result, only one of the host's children was able to sit with us for dinner. After about ten minutes, the eldest child got up from the table and was quickly replaced by one of their siblings. As I watched the new child at the table eat rapidly, I noticed the other children were waiting for their turn at the table. The oldest children would eat first, while the youngest hoped enough would be left for them when their turn came.

Many emotions flooded my mind that day as I gazed into the eyes of the waiting children. At first, I was angry with my host for implementing a system where the youngest and most vulnerable children would eat last, but self-conviction quickly consumed me. I put down my fork and left the table, which allowed a child to take *my* place. I wasn't overeating by Western standards, but I certainly didn't need to continue. Had I perceived the situation sooner, I would have gladly gone without a meal that night. The more I consumed, the less food the children received. That was a lesson in perspective that I have never forgotten.

Imagine yourself sitting in a chair and attempting to remain perfectly still. No matter how hard you try, you will not succeed because you will always be moving at breakneck speed. You see, the earth completes one complete rotation in just under twenty-four hours. Since the circumference of the planet is about forty thousand kilometers, the surface of the earth at the equator is moving at a speed of four hundred sixty meters per second, roughly one thousand miles per hour.[1] Your previous viewpoint wasn't necessarily wrong, but you didn't have a full perspective. As Christians, we need to look "higher" as we ask the Lord for the correct perception of the situations we face.

In 2 Kings 6:8, we read the story of Elisha the prophet being trapped by the army of Aram. Elisha was able to discern the battle plans of the Arameans supernaturally and was revealing them to the King of Israel. The King of Aram came by night and encircled the city of Dothan, where Elisha and his servant were sleeping.

When they awoke the next morning, the servant looked out the window and saw the siege against the city. "'Oh no, my lord! What shall we do?'" he asked.[2] They were completely surrounded, with no chance of escape, and thoughts of death and torture were probably flooding the servant's mind. Did he regret trying to live the godly lifestyle that ultimately took him to that place of destruction?

Elisha, however, was unfazed. "'Do not be afraid,' the prophet answered. 'Those who are with us are more than those who are with them.'"[3] He knew he'd followed the Lord's will and his God would protect them. Feelings are powerful, but they are often misleading. The servant was focused on the earthly circumstances, but Elisha saw a broader perspective. Even when the "crowd" was against them, Elisha looked higher.

He remained calm and focused because that's what leaders do. He didn't get frustrated or upset, which allowed him to see what was necessary. His friend needed prayer. He needed a different vantage point.

> "Oh Lord, please open his eyes that he may see." So the Lord opened the eyes of the young man and he saw, and behold, the mountain was full of horses and chariots of fire all around Elisha.
>
> — 2 Kgs 6:17 ESV

Being at peace allows us the margin to pray for the peace of others. If our minds are clouded by the complexity of the problems that seem to envelop us, how can we possibly be part of the solution? All we can do is contribute to the noise.

But I wonder if Elisha saw the army of the Lord the entire time or if he just *knew* it to be true? Do we need to see with our earthly eyes before we believe the Lord will protect us? Will we let the pain of the past affect our perspective of the future?

My trip to Tanzania taught me that no matter how dire my circumstances may seem, someone else has a harder obstacle. That does not diminish the emotion of my challenges, but it should give me perspective. That is exactly what Elisha was teaching his servant.

We *do* know that Elisha was familiar with flaming chariots because his mentor, Elijah, had been taken away in one.[4] Losing a close friend or family member is never easy, and that gave Elisha every opportunity for offense. The very sight of the Lord's chariots would have brought back bitter memories. Like Elisha, we must decide whether we will be governed by our past or our future. Do we trust the Lord's timing and provision?

It comes down to one simple question: do you believe your life is surrounded by the Lord or by the crowd? Will you be overwhelmed by the problems in the world, or will you be overwhelmed with the Lord's love? To which voice will you listen?

As the Aramean army advanced on the city, Elisha prayed for them to be blinded. In other words, he wanted them to lose their current (incorrect) perspective. He did not ask for their destruction. In fact, he led them deep into the land of Samaria before he prayed for their eyes to be opened. He then displayed compassion and instructed the King of Israel to feed and care for them. This was a terrible military strategy! Anyone focused on winning a battle would not have hesitated to destroy their enemies. But Elisha was not concentrating on earthly conflict. He was devoted to a much different confrontation. "For the weapons of our warfare are not of the flesh but have divine power to destroy strongholds."[5]

The Bible says that from that day onward, Aram never raided the land of Israel again. Something had changed. Elisha was able to rise above the problems that surrounded him and bring peace, not only to himself and his servant, but to both warring nations. He rose above his circumstances and got a higher perspective.

You may not find yourself in the middle of military conflict, but you may be facing other challenges. The solution to your conflict can be difficult to see, but it may be much different than you imagine. Elisha teaches us that there is a peace that comes to those who seek the higher perspective. It's there that we discover our problems are much smaller than they appear.

13

FAMILY DRAMA (GEN 25–33)

Esau and his brother Jacob were twins. They wrestled in the womb and would struggle with each other for their entire lives. Jacob came into this world clutching his brother's heel, which became the metaphor for his name and his life—Jacob was a deceiver.

He was a quiet man, preferring the kitchen over the fields, and he developed a close relationship with his mother, Rebekah. The opposite was true for his brother Esau, who once came in from a long hunting trip and sold his birthright to Jacob for a single bowl of stew.[1] Esau was a man who forged his own destiny and didn't cling to inheritance or entitlement. He was a man's man, covered in thick hair and carrying the aroma of the forest. He discovered the way to his father's heart was through his stomach and thus became his favorite son.

When their father Isaac was old and his eyes were failing, he wanted to give his eldest son the traditional blessing. While Esau was hunting for the ceremonial dinner, his mother, Rebekah, crafted an elaborate ruse. She covered her beloved younger son Jacob with animal hair and gave him a dinner to take to his father. Since Isaac could not see, he relied on his senses of touch and smell to identify which of his sons was before him. In that way, Jacob played the deceiver once again and stole his brother's blessing. When Esau returned and learned what Jacob had done, he vowed in his mind to take revenge: "'The days of mourning for my father are approaching; then I will kill my brother Jacob.'"[2]

Fearing reprisal, Jacob fled to his mother's brother in the land of Haran, where he spent two decades avoiding his problems. He fell in love with a woman named Rachel and agreed to work seven years in exchange for her hand in marriage. But when the wedding night came, Jacob was the one deceived. His Uncle Laban had tricked him into marrying his elder daughter, Leah, instead of Rachel.

Jacob was in bed with the wrong sister and somehow didn't notice. Was he so focused on achieving the milestones of life that he failed to notice the people he was using to get there? The pattern of brokenness was multiplying, but Jacob wasn't ready to address the root cause. He was angry with Laban for the wedding deception and failed to see the ironic connection to his own duplicity. Families can be like that, with each person holding onto years of offense but neglecting to recognize their own role in the story. We tend to underestimate the portion of the blame that belongs to us while over-magnifying what others have done.

Laban gave Jacob both daughters in exchange for seven more years of service. The Lord blessed Laban because of Jacob, and the size of his sheep herds greatly increased. He struck a deal with his uncle and father-in-law on how they would split the wealth, but once again, Jacob needed to twist the system. He shrewdly manipulated the mating of the animals so that he received most of the herd. He knew he had cheated Laban just as he had deceived Esau, and just like with his brother, he fled without a word.

How you leave each season in life will impact the trajectory of your future. Whether switching jobs or leaving a church, there is a proper way to move on. However, many people use their new opportunity as an occasion to blow up the bridge of relationship in spectacular fashion. Why would someone write a venting letter to their former pastor, describing all the ways the church had failed them? What causes the employee to make sure everyone knows their previous work environment was toxic? The answer is insecurity. Leaving doesn't fix the issue when you are causing the problem.

Confrontation was not something Jacob did well, but Laban forced the issue when he pursued them. Jacob blamed his father-in-law for being the dishonest one and justified his actions by pointing toward the Lord's blessing as validation.[3] He also turned the hearts of Rachel and Leah away from their father, continuing his pattern of relational division. Jacob had a history of causing family drama, and his dishonesty infected Rachel, who stole some of her father's belongings.[4] Laban had benefited from over twenty years of Jacob's labor and had certainly not been completely fair, but the path to your future is always limited by the way you leave each stage along the way.

Jacob had daddy issues and a deep-seated resentment of living in the shadow of his brother. He believed his uncle had tricked him, cheated him, and squandered twenty years of his life. He was justified because he was the victim. But a voice penetrated the pain and said, "'Go back to the land of your fathers and relatives, and I will be with you.'"[5] Jacob needed to stop running and face the consequences of his actions.

Knowing Esau would be waiting for him, Jacob sent numerous gifts in advance, hoping to quench his brother's thirst for revenge. For years, he had strived and connived in his pursuit of material possessions, so why did he send these livestock and servants to Esau as a present? Was he trying to return some of the blessing he had stolen from his brother so many years before? Was he finally admitting his empty pursuit of the things of this world?

Esau ignored the tokens and went to meet Jacob with four hundred armed men. That was the pivotal moment when Jacob needed to decide whether he would be defined by his past or his future as a lifetime of fear was collapsing upon him. He came into this world holding the heel of his twin brother and had spent his life scheming to regain the lead.

He came to the Jordan River, the metaphorical line of demarcation between bondage and blessing. He sent his family and possessions across while he stayed alone and wrestled with his God. Jacob struggled all night and, in the end, came to the conclusion that the one thing he would not give up was the blessing of the Lord. That was the moment he let go of all the other things in his life, and his destiny changed.

> "Your name shall no longer be called Jacob, but Israel; for you have struggled with God and with men, and have prevailed."
>
> — Gen 32:28 NKJV

In his dream, the Lord grabbed his hip to force Jacob to let go, and for the rest of his life, he would walk with a limp, never forgetting the moment that God profoundly touched his life.

As he approached Esau the next morning, Jacob was finally free to make peace with his past. He simply bowed before his brother and accepted the consequences of his actions. But Esau ran to meet his brother and threw his arms around him. He'd missed Jacob and longed for the family reunion that could have occurred many years before, if not for Jacob's self-inflicted exile.

Unforgiveness is a prison in which we keep ourselves. It's a place of deception in which we believe we're exacting revenge on someone by holding onto bitterness and pain. But in reality, the other person moves on with their life, often without any knowledge or understanding of what is taking place in our minds. Jacob spent twenty years believing he could not go home, while during that entire time, his family was longing for his return.

We all grow up in imperfect households where the rough edges of selfishness will cause wounds and scars, but the concept of "family" was God's idea. It's the place where we learn to love and forgive. You may not always agree with everyone in your life, but the value of your relationships transcends all earthly issues. Is it time for you to mend a fence and "return home" like Jacob? Are you willing to put your opinions and politics to the side, focusing instead on what unites you? The pain of your past may be very real, but like Jacob discovered on the shores of the Jordan River, the only thing that matters is the blessing of the Lord.

14

GUARDED TREASURE (2 KGS 18–20)

Israel had been delivered from the bondage of foreign lands but never removed them from their hearts. The conquering people treated the worship of the Lord as a means to an end, one god among many. Forsaking the covenant they'd made with the Lord, they bowed down to other things and sacrificed their faith on the altar of ideology.

> Even while these people were worshipping the Lord, they were serving their idols.
>
> — 2 Kgs 17:41 NIV

During this cultural implosion, only the land of Judah remained free as Israel was subjected to the rule of the Assyrian Empire. In the year 739 BC, a prince was born in Jerusalem by the name of Hezekiah. He was not the firstborn son, for his older brother had been burned alive in a pagan ritual by his father King Ahaz.[1] At the age of twenty-five, Hezekiah became king of Judah and removed all the pagan idols his father had created.

One of the things he destroyed was the bronze pole Moses had lifted up in the desert during the Exodus when the people were bitten by poisonous snakes. All who looked upon it would receive healing,[2] but the source of the power was never the pole —it was simply foreshadowing when the Messiah would be lifted up on the cross.[3] For seven hundred years, the serpent pole remained a symbol of misplaced faith. It had come to be called Nehushtan, obscuring the name of the God who truly heals.

But we should be cautious to judge the actions of the Israelites until we examine our own hearts. Do we trust in our Lord for healing, or do we allow the doctrine of the prevailing culture to persuade us to create idols in our hearts? Has three thousand years made any difference if crystals hang in car windows or believers find entertainment in horoscopes? What you feed will prosper, and what you starve will die.[4] Hezekiah made a decision to remove the things that had blocked access to the one true God.

Before Hezekiah turned forty years old, he was forced to give the king of Assyria all the treasures of the temple in Jerusalem, but this did not appease the Assyrian commander. As the armies laid siege to Jerusalem, the king shouted over the city walls, "'Do not let Hezekiah deceive you for he will not be able to deliver you out of my hand... Make peace with me and come out.'"[5] One hundred eighty-five thousand troops were testing the strength of the foundation of Israel. Hezekiah went before the Lord, and his prayer was heard. That night, the angel of the Lord destroyed the entire Assyrian army.

Time passed, and Hezekiah became ill and was on the threshold of death. The prophet Isaiah came to him and told him to put his house in order. As the dying king poured out his heart, the Lord heard his prayer and extended his life by fifteen years. He asked the Lord for a sign, and the sun moved backward on the sundial ten steps. Hezekiah was overjoyed as he entertained international emissaries who came to see evidence of the miraculous healing.

One of the delegations came from the distant land of Babylon. A sixteen-hundred-mile journey was rewarded by being given a personal tour of all the treasures of the palace. Hezekiah showed them everything private, leaving no secret unshared. That's something kings just do not do, but Hezekiah let down his guard and assumed the Babylonians lived too far away to cause Judah any harm. He didn't seek the heart of the God who had healed him, and his mistake would lead to the suffering of millions.

The Lord sent Isaiah back to Hezekiah with a strong rebuke. "'The time will surely come when everything in your palace, and all that your predecessors have stored up until this day, will be carried off to Babylon. Nothing will be left, says the Lord. And some of your descendants... will be taken away, and they will be eunuchs in the palace of the king of Babylon.'"[6] That was terrible news. Hezekiah's lack of judgement would result in the destruction of Judah and the exile of his ancestors. You would think Hezekiah would be shaken by the information and ask the Lord for mercy, but his response was quite the opposite.

> "The word of the Lord you have spoken is good," Hezekiah replied. For he thought, "Will there not be peace and security in my lifetime?"
>
> — 2 Kgs 20:19 NIV

Hezekiah had witnessed an amazing miracle of healing and been given a supernatural sign that God was with him. The Lord was testing his heart.[7] What will our reaction be when we see the Lord working in our lives? Will we become blind to the blessings and compromise the treasures we've been given? Hezekiah had a chance to be great, but he was limited by his selfishness.

During the extra fifteen years of Hezekiah's life, he had a son named Manasseh, who would become one of the most evil kings in the history of Israel and Judah. The legacy of Hezekiah was short-lived as Manasseh undid all the reforms of his father. That makes you wonder if the extension to Hezekiah's life was really something for which he should have prayed. Sometimes it's the mercy of the Lord not to answer our prayers.

About one hundred years later, King Nebuchadnezzar II laid siege to Jerusalem, and Judah fell into the hands of the Babylonians in 597 BC. The final blow came in 586 BC when the temple and all the important buildings were burned to the ground, and the city walls were destroyed.[8] All the treasures Hezekiah had shown to the Babylonians were carried off to a foreign land. That was the end of the story for Hezekiah, but not for the people of Israel.

The throne room is the center of the kingdom, where the ruler is at their most powerful. For the modern-day believer, this can serve as a metaphor for wherever we derive our strength. When Hezekiah let foreigners into his palace, he let down his guard and compromised his legacy. He grew arrogant because of the miraculous extension to his life and assumed nothing could harm him.

What lesson will you learn from the life of Hezekiah? Will you allow your throne room to be exposed by compromising with the culture around you? Will you measure success by what happens *to* you or by what happens *through* you? Like Hezekiah thousands of years ago, our legacy pivots on the daily decision to guard our hearts and seek the Lord in the only throne room that matters.

15

THE FIRE OF CONVICTION (DANIEL 1–3)

King Hezekiah entertained envoys from Babylon and showed them all the treasures of the land. The prophet Isaiah foretold that this would lead to the destruction of Judah,[1] and within one hundred years, the armies of Nebuchadnezzar took Jerusalem.[2] "'And some of your descendants, your own flesh and blood who will be born to you, will be taken away, and they will become eunuchs in the palace of the king of Babylon.'"[3] This is how Daniel, Hananiah, Mishael, and Azariah came to live in the land of Babylon.

One night, King Nebuchadnezzar had a disturbing dream and summoned all the astrologers to give the interpretation. But the convocation would contain a twist. The king required them to use their powers to tell him the dream itself along with the interpretation. The magicians and sorcerers were terrified at the request, but Daniel had great insight and volunteered for the impossible task. During the night, God, the revealer of mysteries, appeared to Daniel and disclosed the dream of the multifaceted statue that foretold the rise and fall of earthly kingdoms. King Nebuchadnezzar was so pleased that he elevated Daniel to a position of power, and Daniel brought along his three friends.

But politics and selfishness have short memories. Despite having been shown the power of the God of the Hebrews, King Nebuchadnezzar erected a massive idol ninety feet high and nine feet wide, ironically reminiscent of the one he saw in his dream. He demanded that at the sound of music, everyone should bow down to the idol under the penalty of death. But the Hebrews reserved their worship for the one true God, and these four men ignored the king's command.

The other officials, jealous of the position of power to which Daniel and his companions had risen, plotted their downfall. King Nebuchadnezzar was enraged when he learned that three of the Hebrew officials had disobeyed his order. He gave them a second chance to comply and avoid being thrown into a blazing furnace. "'Then what god will be able to rescue you from my hand?'"[4]

You may not literally live in the land of Babylon, but you will face social pressures to conform. Modern cultures will allow you to be religious as long as you ultimately bow down to worship their values. In a world that tolerates opinions only until they deviate from the demands of those in power, you must decide which altar will receive your worship.

I find it interesting that we more commonly know Daniel's friends by their Babylonian names of Shadrach, Meshach, and Abednego whereas Daniel's Babylonian name of Belteshazzar[5] is more obscure. The three men were selecting the epitaph of their legacy. Would Shadrach, Meshach and Abednego bow down to the image of gold, or would Hananiah, Mishael, and Azariah trust in the God of Heaven and Earth?

> "[W]e do not need to defend ourselves before you in this matter. If we are thrown into the blazing furnace, the God we serve is able to save us from it, and he will deliver us from Your Majesty's hand. But even if he does not, we want you to know, Your Majesty, that we will not serve your gods or worship the image of gold you have set up."
>
> — Dan 3:16-18 NIV

Many scholars have pointed at this passage as the

articulation of faith—to be confident that the Lord is in control irrespective of any earthly outcome. The three friends were so firmly focused on the reality of the Kingdom of God that they were unmoved by the earthly perspective. Indeed, faith is being sure of what we hope for and certain of what we cannot see.[6] Theirs was more than just a religious opinion—it was a deep-seated conviction.

A big difference exists between opinions and convictions. Opinions are preferences in a continuum of options. *What is your favorite color? What kind of food do you like?* But convictions are rooted in your conscience. You can easily change your opinions over time, but you cannot alter your convictions without changing who you are. So while you may hold onto your opinions, your convictions hold onto you.[7]

Hananiah, Mishael, and Azariah were not able to give up their beliefs despite the political opinions of the powers that surrounded them. Their focus was on the Lord, not the politics of the land. They were at peace with giving up their lives because they knew the source of true life. They had no interest in politics even if those methods would help accomplish godly things on earth.

King Nebuchadnezzar was furious and ordered the furnace heated seven times hotter than normal. They were bound with ropes and thrown into the flames, which were so intense that the guards were incinerated. But as the king looked into the fire, he was amazed to see four figures walking around unharmed, and the fourth looked like a son of the gods.

King Nebuchadnezzar called them forth from the fire, and everyone crowded around them. They had not been harmed and had no odor of smoke on their bodies. This is a picture of how we are called to live in the earthly cultures that surround us. We may find ourselves in difficult circumstances and feel the pressure to conform, but when we come out of the fires of the world, what will we smell like? Will we be "the aroma of Christ to God among those who are being saved and among those who are perishing?"[8] Or will we compromise our faith so that it aligns with the prevailing winds of opinion?

You must be very careful not to turn your convictions into weaponized opinions, for that would be playing the political war games of the nations surrounding you. If the convictions of the believer are not grounded in love, the aroma of their dogma becomes a stench that repulses the very people they are called to reach.

Nebuchadnezzar said, "'Praise be to the God of Shadrach, Meshach and Abednego, who has sent his angel and rescued his servants! They trusted in him and defied the king's command and were willing to give up their lives rather than serve or worship any god except their own God.'"[9] Again they were promoted and eventually forgotten. Their goal was never to gain favor with the king. They simply wanted to live for the Lord. Their lives remain a witness and an example that has challenged many generations.

Whom will you serve? Standing up for your creed is easy when the flames are low, but what will you do when the people around you demand that you comment on their narrative and embrace their passion? Will you use their tactics to defend yourself, or will you keep your eyes on the revealer of mysteries? When you feel like you're in the middle of the fire, will you be able to walk unharmed? If you end up in the middle of the flames, know that someone else is in there with you. The world will be changed when people of conviction are more aware of the Lord than the storms that rage around them.

16

DROWNING IN NOISE (MATT 14:22–34)

Jesus made the disciples get into a boat and head to the opposite side of the Sea of Galilee. He wouldn't be going with them in the vessel because he was staying to dismiss the crowd of thousands that had gathered to hear the words of life. The disciples had witnessed an amazing miracle when Jesus had multiplied five loaves and two fish. What was going through their minds as they took turns rowing into the darkening skies? They'd seen the Lord provide for other people, but would their faith endure in the midst of their own need?

After Jesus dismissed the people, he went up on the mountainside to pray. This had been his goal prior to the crowds arriving, and he was returning to his original task. The moments life seems too busy to pray is when we most need to make that time.

Prayer is a deliberate action to separate ourselves

from the daily confusion that surrounds us. We eliminate the distractions and seek to hear what the Lord has to say. Sometimes silence is the best answer because it reminds us that many of our questions are just noise. Jesus just wanted to pray. He needed to pray. He reminds us that we need to stop because the needs of the world never will.

The rest of the story is a living metaphor. You and I are in that boat as modern-day disciples. Like them, we may be struggling, buffeted by headwinds and with a considerable distance remaining to the safety of the shore. The Lord might seem absent when the storm clouds start closing in.

In the middle of the night, when life was at its darkest, Jesus came to them, walking on the water. But they did not recognize him, mistaking him for a ghostly apparition. Why is it that people are so open to the existence of ghosts but unwilling to embrace the concept of God? Faith is easy, right up to the point where it makes a demand upon your life.

Immediately, Jesus reassures them, "'It's me—don't be afraid.'"[1] Each of them was faced with a decision—to which sounds would they listen? Waves were splashing in their faces and wind blowing their hair. The smell of the sea and swirling waves would have captured all their senses. The storms of life are real, and some are very large. In the midst of all the noise surrounding us, will we hear the calling of the Lord?

Then Peter does the unthinkable. He asks Jesus to allow him to walk on the water. Great devotion is necessary for one to inquire and even greater faith to step out. I wonder if any of the other disciples warned Peter not to try or if anyone else wanted to follow but was paralyzed by fear. Why was Peter the only one to reposition himself? The storm was big, but Jesus was bigger.

Peter was defying the laws of physics as he focused on the one who'd created them. The first step is hard, but you still have one foot in the boat. Taking that second step is when your commitment is tested. Will we gain confidence as we follow the Lord or let the cacophony convince us to focus on other things?

Suddenly Peter was sinking and falling into the raging sea. The voice of the Lord faded as Peter sank like the rock for which he was named. The noise of the storm surrounding the boat soon became more real than the miraculous act of walking on the water. But Jesus saved Peter, both in the storm and on the cross.

The world around us can seem like a raging sea of political and social crises. The problems we face are large and complex, and those who seek to solve those issues need our prayers and support. But as an individual, will you find that place of peace that allows you to hear the sound of the Lord above the storm? If your life is in chaos, how can you bring peace to those that need it? Anger and offense sell newspapers and attract readers but end up causing more problems than they solve. The world doesn't need more yelling. It needs people who are like Jesus. He sought a solitary place where he could pray in quiet, that place of perspective that allows us to see the approaching crowd as people, not problems—to meet the needs that come our way then return to that place of prayer to refocus on the solution giver.

The storms of life will rage, but the word of the Lord is always present even though we might not perceive it. "'You of little faith, why did you doubt?'"[2] Don't let the chorus of problems become louder than the invitation bidding you to come. The Lord allowed the storm, but he did not cause it. The influence of the naysayers was what needed to drown, not Peter. Will you have the courage to lower the volume of the distractions and listen for the only voice that matters?

17

DO YOU WANT TO GET WELL? (JOHN 5:1–15)

This was the disciples' first trip to Jerusalem as a group, and Jesus had performed only two miracles prior to arriving. The Pool of Bethesda lay inside the city walls, and a great number of disabled people would lie nearby and wait for the waters to stir, believing that the first person to get into the basin would be healed of their illness. I wonder if anyone had ever been healed in this manner. Some shred of truth must have existed in the tales—why else would so many people have kept trying? Then again, people often get stuck in a pattern of thinking regardless of its outcome.

We know Jesus had the power to heal everyone at the pool that day, but he did not. We also know that Jesus had lots of things to accomplish while he was in Jerusalem, yet he chose to linger and inquire about the people that were gathered. He learned that one man had been lying there for thirty-eight years and asked him a simple but painful question: "'Do you want to get well?'"[1]

The world has no shortage of problems, and many people have found themselves victimized by the actions of others. Systemic issues exist in every culture that make meaningful change difficult to reach the edges of a society. I don't want to trivialize any of these challenges nor suggest that every situation simply requires a change of thinking. In other words, this isn't an attempt at a blanket solution or public policy statement. This is simply the story of what was holding one man back from his destiny.

The man was quick to list off excuses because he was convinced that the root cause of his continued infirmity didn't rest with him. "'I have no one to help me into the pool when the water is stirred.'"[2] Was it really true that this man had no friends, or had he grown blind in addition to being crippled? Our modern society is increasingly lonelier, and technology has redefined what it means to be a "friend," but it takes being a friend to get a friend.

Maybe this man's support group had thinned over his thirty-eight years of playing the victim. Being around offense is hard. Every topic somehow ends up reverting back to unmet needs and how no one has come to offer assistance. No matter how hard one tries to help someone in this condition, nothing ever seems quite good enough for them. Inquiries aren't reciprocated because the focus is always one-sided. After thirty-eight years of this man being paralyzed and in the same spot in life, it would have been surprising if he *did* have any friends.

A day comes when each of us must take responsibility for the decisions that have caused us to end up at our own Pool of Bethesda, that place where we make excuses for no longer trying as hard as we did in the past. This was clearly the inference of the question Jesus asked, and it led to the second most popular excuse: "'While I am trying to get in, someone else goes down ahead of me.'"[3] Jealousy is a short commute from the crowded streets of self-pity.

> "Get up! Pick up your mat and walk."
>
> —John 5:8 NIV

Three simple instructions from the mouth of Jesus guided this man to freedom. First, get up. Stop sitting in the same spot and expecting a different result. Rehashing the pain that got you to this point will never help you move on. Next, pick up your mat. Don't expect someone else to get it for you. And thirdly, the time to walk is long overdue, to move on from this season of life in which you've given up on thriving, being content to simply survive. These were the lifesaving words of Jesus that forced the man to decide where he would place his identity.

If you examine the text carefully, the man was cured, *then* he picked up his mat and walked. This means that he had already stood up before Scripture declared him cured. He decided he wanted to get well and proclaimed it by standing. He rose past the inertia of the past and found freedom in his obedience to the words of Jesus.

We are called human *beings*, not human *doings*. Our identities are to be found in who we are, not in what we can accomplish on Earth. But we can fall into the trap of focusing on our problems and, over time, begin to find identity in our failures to the point that we can perpetuate our conditions.

Blaming other people for problems is easy, demanding them to provide solutions. We expect those with more resources to donate to charity and governments to provide helpful programs, but focusing on people as your solution can obscure the root issue. If you want to get well, maybe you need to get up and walk. Perhaps the only thing keeping you from your breakthrough is the misguided assumption that your current season is the final chapter in your story.

I recall a time in my life when I was playing football as a teenager. Several times, I was tackled with such force that it knocked the wind from my lungs, leaving me depleted on the ground. Everything within me was screaming to stay down, and I was tempted to quit and wait for medical attention to remove me from the field. But I made a decision in each moment of pain and chose to stand up. The details of those incidents are still vivid in my mind even thirty years later. When the events of life have threatened to keep me down, I recall the lesson I learned on the field—I might not be able to control what knocks me down in life, but I always have the choice to rise.

Not every challenge is as simple as my example, and I don't want to trivialize circumstances with which I'm not personally acquainted. But I also know that God is bigger than any earthly challenge and is able to meet every need. If you're struggling in a difficult season in life and find yourself stuck in a pattern of failure, maybe you need to shift your focus away from the obstacles and make a deliberate choice to stand.

18

HOW DID I END UP HERE? (1 KGS 19:1–18)

Rain hadn't fallen in Israel for three years, and Elijah was a wanted man. He was the one who'd predicted the drought and the one that King Ahab blamed for the outcome. Elijah summoned the king to the top of Mt. Carmel, along with eight hundred fifty false prophets appointed by Queen Jezebel. The time had come for the people to decide to whom they would give their allegiance.

Two sacrifices were placed on some wood, one by the prophets and one by Elijah. Everyone would pray, and the one true God would answer with fire. The prophets of Baal went first. For hours, they cut themselves in a pagan ritual as they shouted to their god, but Baal was silent. Elijah quietly went next, dousing the wood in water for extra emphasis. With a simple word, he called on the Lord, who answered in dramatic fashion. Fire fell from heaven, consuming not only the sacrifice, but the stones, soil, and even the water. Nobody doubted that day that the Lord was the God of Heaven and Earth. The false prophets were executed, and Ahab returned to the city to tell the queen what had happened to her prophets.

Jezebel sent word to Elijah, "'May the gods deal with me, be it ever so severely, if by this time tomorrow I do not make your life like that of one of them.'"[1] The Bible says that when Elijah heard the queen's message, he was scared and ran for his life. The mighty prophet that had called down fire from heaven saw something and was afraid of it. He ran about one hundred miles from Jezreel to Beersheba, where he lay down under a tree and prayed to die.

> "I've had enough, Lord. Take my life; I am no better than my ancestors."
>
> — 1 Kgs 19:4 NIV

Can you relate to wanting to give up? Have you ever asked the Lord for a sign that he is real? If you had witnessed the fire fall from heaven, would you have doubted that God was in control of your life? The scene on Mount Carmel is viewed by many people as the culmination of Elijah's ministry, but sometimes the mountaintop of success seems different once we get there.

Fear is faith in reverse. It sees the problem whereas faith sees the solution giver. How could Elijah doubt the supernatural protection of the Lord after Mount Carmel? But are we any different from Elijah? We doubt God's goodness toward us, not necessarily his power. We know he can—we're just not sure if he will.

Elijah was tired of running. He was tired of motivating the people to serve the Lord. He fell asleep under the tree and was prepared to die, when an angel woke him and gave him some food. This was repeated a second time before Elijah had enough energy to travel about two hundred sixty miles to Mount Horeb. The Bible says he traveled for forty days and forty nights, which could be hyperbole, or it could mean that he traveled very slowly.

Why did Elijah go to this mountain? Scholars believe Mt. Horeb and Mt. Sinai were two different names for the same location, perhaps describing the two sides of the mountain, depending on your direction.[2] That was where Moses first met the Lord at the burning bush.[3] At the bottom of that mountain, the Israelites built the Golden Calf while Moses and Joshua met with God.[4] There, Moses received the Ten Commandments[5] and struck the rock to give water to the people,[6] and there the Israelites eventually made their final turn toward the Promised

Land.[7] But that was also the place where God hid Moses in the cleft of the rock when his glory passed.[8] Was Elijah running away, or was he traveling to the one place on earth where he knew he could hear from God?

Elijah reached the mountain and spent the night in a cave. The word of the Lord came to him: "'What are you doing here, Elijah?'"[9]

Life is full of twists and turns. We set out in a certain direction with goals and dreams, but sometimes we end up in places we did not expect. Can you relate to the soul-searching that Elijah must have been doing? *How did I end up here?*

We make excuses because the fault is obviously not ours. Elijah said, "'I have been very zealous for the Lord God Almighty. The Israelites have rejected your covenant, broken down your altars, and put your prophets to death with the sword. I am the only one left, and now they are trying to kill me too.'"[10]

The Lord told Elijah to stand on the mountain, just as Moses had done so many years before. A great and powerful wind tore the rocks from the surface of the hill, but the Lord was not in the wind. After the wind came an earthquake then a fire, but the Lord was not in those either. Then came a gentle whisper, the still small voice of the Lord. When Elijah heard it, he knew he was standing in the presence of the Creator. Again came the question, "'What are you doing here?'"[11] followed by the same excuses.

The Lord is patient, but he does not compromise. He is compassionate and is your biggest cheerleader. "'For I know the plans I have for you,' declares the Lord, 'plans to... give you hope and a future.'"[12] We must recognize the mistakes that contributed to our present condition in order to leave it behind. Your future is not dependent on what brought you here but rather on what you do from this moment onward.

The Lord told Elijah, "'Go back the way you came.'"[13] Sometimes, the shortest path involves a little backtracking. We all need mountaintop experiences, but faith is forged in the valley. As Moses had done four hundred years prior,[14] Elijah had stayed on this mountain long enough; the time had come to break camp and move on.

Things happen in our lives for lots of reasons. Some are good, and some are not so good. Sometimes, we end up paying the consequences of our own mistakes, and other times, we are on the receiving end of a mistake made by someone else. But the Lord will never be surprised or caught off guard about what happens to you. "All the days ordained for me were written in your book before one of them came to be."[15] He has known the end from the beginning.[16]

We cannot dwell on how we ended up here—we must change our perceptions and consider the purpose for the next steps he wants us to make. This may be a bad chapter, but it's not the end of the book. All these things that have happened are just context for the amazing things your future contains. This is all just scenery for the exciting conclusion of your blessing.

Whether Elijah was fleeing from his problems or running after his Lord depends on one's perspective, but either motivation involved the same road. Though our earthly journey contains mountains and valleys, that doesn't negate the Lord's presence in our lives. Sometimes, we just need to pause long enough to hear his reassuring whisper that we are right where he needs us to be.

19

MINISTERS OF RECONCILIATION (2 COR 5:14–21)

Several years ago, I was working with a man who sent off a blistering email to many of my coworkers, accusing me of attacking his work. His was an emotionally charged personal affront that was not based in fact. I didn't know him well and considered distancing myself to protect my career from potential sabotage. I also thought about escalating the situation to senior management by reporting the conduct of my coworker. But the Lord has called me to be a minister of reconciliation, and that doesn't exclude the secular workplace.

I sent the man a private note and asked him if he was okay. I showed compassion toward him and ignored all the things he'd said in his public email. Apparently, his grandmother was dying, and the rest of the family was in bitter conflict. The tone of my response defused his aggression and enabled him to see that he had treated me poorly. He apologized to me and became a friend and ally. When we choose the path of peace, we become the solution and stop the multiplication of offense.

Paul addresses this topic in his second letter to the Corinthians. Evidence in the epistles suggests that factions in Corinth were causing division and personally attacking Paul's ministry. He chose to pass up opportunities to preach the Gospel in other regions because he wanted to personally address the situation in Corinth.[1] "[H]e has committed to us the message of reconciliation. We are therefore Christ's ambassadors, as though God were making his appeal through us," Paul wrote.[2] When you see fragmentation, it's your calling as a Christian to sow seeds of solidarity.

> "Christ's love compels us, because we are convinced that he died for all"—even the people with whom we disagree.
>
> — 2 Cor 5:14 NIV

That includes individuals that attack us or try to bring us down and who possess personalities that are difficult to love. When Jesus looked at the sin of the world, he embraced the cross and died for people to be made whole. When we are confronted with that same sin, what will be our reaction? Will we crusade against the sinner? Will we view it as an attack on the moral fabric of our nation and a violation of the principles of our founding fathers? Will we declare our anger to be righteous and justify the way we lash out at those with a different worldview? If someone read your social media feed, would they come to the conclusion that you're a minister of reconciliation or an agent of division?

This passage is very clear. Verse 15 says we should no longer live for ourselves but for him who died for them and was raised again. And according to verse 16, we should regard no one from a worldly point of view. We are new creations. The old has gone, and the new has come.[3] Just as Christ reconciled us to God, so also our lives should be devoted to the mediation of people, not the widespread adoption of a moral code. When we focus on rules, our hearts grow callous to the people that Christ died to save.

Have you ever been sent an email with a large distribution list, in which the sender forgot to use the blind carbon copy (BCC) feature? Inevitably, someone responds to the entire group with a message like "Please take me off this list." This, of course, causes other people to respond with the same message. Soon, your email inbox is blowing up with exponentially increasing advice for everyone to stop replying to the entire group. Each new email is not a solution—it perpetuates the problem.

Pain is like that. People lash out at other people because they are in pain. But when they do, this creates new offense that causes additional victims to react in unkind ways. It's a vicious cycle that has no end until someone decides to stop the ripple effect. True change occurs when we rise above the battle and choose the path of peace.

It has been said that "hurt people hurt people." Defusing a situation starts with an introspective consideration of our own heart. *How have I hurt other people and brought them pain?* What is your role in the perpetuation of the wounds swirling in your life? This may be a very difficult proposition to consider, but I promise that your very life depends on it. You might have been the victim of the extreme selfishness and vindictiveness of another soul, but that doesn't define you. Your Lord died for that pain, and he is calling you to be his ambassador of reconciliation.

When someone attacks us, Jesus calls us to see their anguish rather than the trouble they're inflicting. The Lord modeled this attitude on the cross when he said, "'Father, forgive these people! They don't know what they're doing.'"[4] From now on, each of us has a choice. Will our lives be marked by discord or harmony?

Jesus was a champion of those who have no

voice. He visited the homes of "sinners" and the outcasts of society and was not afraid to grasp the untouchables as he healed them of leprosy. He elevated the role of women in a patriarchal period of history, challenged the scourge of racism, and embraced those of a different lineage. But in every situation, he sought community, not isolation. He never tore down but only built up. And when the world's system came against him, he didn't fight back—he willingly chose the cross. Your godly passion may be stoked for a worthy cause, but your behavior is what communicates the message of reconciliation.

20

WHO IS MY NEIGHBOR? (LUKE 10:25–37)

"On one occasion an expert in the law stood up to test Jesus."[1] The man was already convinced he knew the answer and was confident he was the expert. His question was timeless, asked by many seekers and skeptics throughout history.

"What must I do to inherit eternal life?"

— Luke 10:25 NIV

Some people ask this question because they doubt such a place exists, while others don't want to miss out on their eternal reward. But the question itself is inappropriate for a Christian because our salvation manifests not in what we *do* but in who we *become* along the way.

Jesus responds by asking a question of his own: "'What do the Scriptures say?'"[2] The man was an expert in the Law—the *do*s and *don't*s of the Hebrew religion. Certainly, he would have read Scripture many times, but had the truth of the writing pervaded his beliefs? I believe the Lord would ask all of us this same question: what does the Scripture say?

Years ago, I was in an animated discussion with a person who had a very strong opinion on an extremely controversial social topic. We disagreed, but we both claimed to be Christians. I asked him if he could support his points from any verses in the Bible. His response still echoes in my heart: "I don't care what God says." Those were his exact words. As a believer, are you already convinced you have the correct perspective on social topics, or are you open to seeking what the Lord has to say on any given subject?

The man in our story knew the truth. He just wasn't living it. Love God and love people—that is the mission statement for our lives. Everything else sorts itself out when we live by those simple words. Seeing life through the lens of other people removes any notion of selfishness. But the man wanted to justify himself. He was convinced that the way he was living was already good enough, so he wouldn't let the Scripture refine his thinking. Thus, he asked Jesus, "'And who is my neighbor?'"[3] Certainly, love has its boundaries, right?

By definition, neighbors are people that are in close proximity and impact your life in some way. As technology makes migration easier, the boundaries between ethnicities increasingly overlap. People with different cultures and backgrounds experience life in intersecting circles. Racism is seeing other people as inferior based on their ethnic differences and is, at its core, a manifestation of selfishness.

Humans have an innate desire to compete. If we don't have everything we think we deserve, we have a tendency to view other people as the cause. But if the Christian believes that God is their source, no room for covetousness should exist. This is the tenth commandment.[4] But all too often, we quantify our jealousy and begin to resent those whom we feel have negatively impacted our lives. When the mind conceives such division along ethnic lines, it gives birth to racism.

Humans are tribal people. From the playground to the workplace, we tend to group ourselves with people that are "like us." In New England, baseball fans are fiercely divided between the Boston Red Sox and the New York Yankees. (The New York Mets fans are innocent bystanders.) If you are not from that part of the world or are not a baseball fan, understanding the depth of this animosity may be hard for you to understand. But at the time of the national elections, those same groups of people form new allegiances to their political parties. This simple example demonstrates that we use arbitrary labels to classify who is on "our team." Given a different context, the coalitions change. People who believe in the same cultural values congregate in similar circles, which can give us a feeling of being "home." But none of those artificial distinctions justify genuine hatred. When we look at Scripture and adjust the context of our classification, we are reminded that we are all brothers and sisters in Christ.

Jesus used a parable to illustrate where this man's thinking had gone wrong. A man had been traveling on a road and fell victim to robbers. They took his possessions, stripped him naked, beat him senseless, and left him like trash along the road. In every way, this man was victimized. Hearing what happened to him causes the desire for justice to rise up within us. The story was meant to trigger emotions, memories of when we might have been victimized. Something deep inside all of us wants to help the man who was robbed, and if we are honest, we hope that the end of the story will bring revenge upon the thieves. But the story Jesus tells goes in a much different direction. Three people come upon the man and have very different reactions—first a priest, then a Levite, and finally, a man from Samaria.

We look up to our ministers as examples of how to live, but this priest avoided the problem, going out of his way to cross to the other side of the road. The man from the privileged tribe of Levi did the same thing, focusing on his own safety and well-being. Jesus did not accidentally use these two personas as the negative examples. The parable was in response to a religious person trying to justify his own lifestyle. If Jesus had given them speaking parts in the story, perhaps they would have asked, "What are we supposed to do? We can't solve all the problems in the world! There is so much injustice, and you can't help every single person in need." But Jesus wasn't talking about the entire world—just one man dying on the road.

We aren't told what type of person was attacked and victimized because that shouldn't matter—people are people. Christians should believe that no life is less important than another—that's what makes us different. One hundred fifty thousand people die every day,[5] but how many of those deaths make the nightly news? Some of those casualties will be labeled a tragedy, while others will be ignored. From the world's perspective, some lives are more important than others.

The third man in the parable was from Samaria, a people group that were victims of prejudice and racial injustice. At the time of Jesus, the Jews viewed the Samaritans as an inferior people that had intermarried with other people groups at the time of the Assyrian invasion in 722 BC. But the Samaritans viewed themselves as the true adherents to the Law of Moses because they had not been deported to Babylon. The Samaritans slowly diminished in numbers over the next two millennia but were a marginalized people at the time of Christ.[6]

When Jesus used a Samaritan as the hero of the story, he was deliberately challenging the racial bias of his listeners. The story could easily have been about a Samaritan being left for dead along the road and a Jewish priest rising above the cultural bias to help someone in need, but Jesus went deeper. How does it feel to have someone whom you despise be the hero in your life? One of the most victimized people was the very person who made the first move to end the division.

The Samaritan bandaged up the man's wounds and took him to the nearest town to get him additional care. He used his own resources to address the injustice and bring peace to the man's life. He even pledged to give additional money when he returned from his own journey. The Samaritan saw this man as his neighbor, someone just like him. He did not see the racial division. More importantly, he didn't let the pain of his own victimization infect his heart.

This is the calling of the Christian, and it should come naturally to us. Love God and love people—that's what we do because of who we are. We must reject the world's narrative that some lives are more important than others. We must dismiss the popular opinions on social issues when they ignore the truth of the Scriptures. We look for the Lord's perspective on who is "on our team" instead of following the patterns of the world around us. The Lord is our source, so no group of people is taking anything away from us. We are the ones that should be champions of diversity rather than division.

21

UNDEBATABLE TRUTH (ACTS 15)

Early in his ministry, the Apostle Paul understood clearly that he was called to bring the light of the Gospel to the nations. The words of Isaiah the prophet resonated with him, providing a mission statement for his life: "'I have made you a light for the Gentiles, that you may bring salvation to the ends of the earth.'"[1] Loving people that society had rejected is something he learned from Barnabas, and together, they saw the Lord move among the Greeks living in Asia Minor. But that ministry would cause friction among the Jewish believers, which soon came to a boiling point.

After traveling over fifteen hundred miles,[2] Paul and Barnabas returned to Antioch in the region of Syria, giving testimony that the people in Asia Minor were openly receptive to the message of the Gospel. When other men came down from Judea to teach that circumcision was necessary for salvation, the two saw an opportunity to influence the church leadership. They both viewed faith in the blood of Jesus as the sole path to heaven for both the Jew and the Gentile. The issue of circumcision was a symptom of a deeper trend of discrimination between the two people groups, being repulsive to the Greeks and exclusive to men of Israel.[3] This was a cultural and religious clash that would become the first doctrinal test of the early church.

The Church in Antioch sent a delegation to meet with the apostles and elders in Jerusalem. The way they handled the situation would determine the trajectory of the movement and would affect the lives of millions of people. Wisdom exists in the abundance of counselors,[4] and seeking life advice can spare us from bad decisions. Many people claim they want to make their own mistakes but then get upset when the consequences occur. Having the right to make your own choices comes with the responsibility of living with the outcome.

If you live in a nation that has won its freedom from an occupying or colonizing force, you probably have a culture that celebrates individual freedom. Patriotism can be a powerful motivator, but it can also have devastating side effects. How you treat people with whom you disagree is a direct reflection of how deeply the love of Christ has penetrated your heart.

In what has become known as the First Council of Jerusalem, the believers entered into a debate. Some who were members of the political party of the Pharisees wanted converts to adhere to the Law of Moses. They stated their case and tried to win over the apostles with their arguments. Paul, himself a former Pharisee, took the dissenting opinion and pleaded the case for Gentiles to not be encumbered with an unnecessary burden.

Peter stood up and addressed the crowd, reminding them of his personal experience in Caesarea, where he was challenged by the Lord on his prejudice against the Gentiles.[5] The Lord had poured out the Holy Spirit on them, just as he had done on the Jewish believers.[6] Peter pointed out to the crowd that God had made no distinction between circumcised and uncircumcised believers.

> "We believe that it is through the grace of our Lord Jesus that we are saved, just as they are."
>
> — ACTS 15:11 NIV

That silenced the crowd. Barnabas and Paul then told an attentive audience about the miraculous signs and wonders done among the Gentiles. No one could argue with the firsthand account that God was moving in the hearts of people far outside the borders of Israel.

During my undergraduate days living on a college campus, I spent many evenings in the dormitories discussing philosophy. Many of those nights were spent with people that prided themselves on being informed and able to quickly dismiss any notions of religious truth. I remember one conversation that took place at a cafeteria table filled with people I didn't know. I was young and insecure, still trying to balance being a Christian on a secular campus. Partway through the meal, one of the others said, "Well, nobody is perfect." To this, for some unknown reason, I felt the need to reply, "Except God."

Immediately, a student named Bill became indignant, loudly proclaiming, "The Bible is full of holes." I found it interesting at the time how he assumed I was talking about the Christian faith and not some other religious concept of God, but being eighteen years old and clearly offended, I decided the debate had begun. I let his words settle for a moment before challenging him to produce an example. "You claim the Bible is full of holes. Can you give five—no, wait —how about three... Make it one example of a contradiction." The entire table shifted their eyes from me back toward Bill like they were watching a tennis match. He grew flustered, and after too much time had passed, he shot back, "The Bible is full of holes!"

The entire table laughed at him, thus giving me my first college debate victory.

In the weeks that followed, Bill never talked to me again. I had won the battle but lost the war. In my own insecurity, I found winning the debate more important than gaining the person. You can argue with abstract ideas because philosophical concepts are for the mind, not the heart. You can debate politics and religion, but you cannot argue with a testimony. That's why Peter and Paul said what they did. They gave a firsthand account of what the Lord had done in and through their lives. We don't need to defend the Lord. We are called only to speak of what he has done in our lives.

James stood up and summarized the decision of the council. The Gentiles would not be required to obey the Law of Moses. Paul and Barnabas were chosen to bring this good news to the Gentile believers around the world, thus launching Paul on his second missionary journey.

The church had weathered its first difference of opinion because they pursued truth over both sides trying to win a debate. This is a timely lesson that modern believers would be wise to learn. The point of a debate is to win, not to seek truth. To win a debate, you need to tell a one-sided account of the facts, omitting anything that might sway opinion against your side of the story.

If we look at the debates in our modern culture,

be it around election time or on social media, people are making the same mistake that I made with Bill. They believe they're showing strength by defending their opinions at all costs, but really, they're just revealing their own insecurity. They wield their arguments like weapons of war, never considering the carnage of their collateral damage. They dehumanize their opponents, failing to see them as people. They get offended and angry, unwilling to step back and see the greater cause. The ability for opposing sides to openly discuss differing ideas has been lost. To debate is to argue, and anger has filled our hearts.

But for the believer, the call is much different. Will you feel the need to rant on your social media page, or will you use your news feed to fuel your prayer list? We are called to be peacemakers, which requires us to rise above cultural noise and be strong enough to listen for the voice of the Lord. Are you trying to win the debate, or will you take the time to seek truth?

22

WORDS MATTER (LUKE 7:18–35)

"Sticks and stones can break my bones, but words will never hurt me." We all knew that playground tune was a lie, but we sang it anyway. We didn't want to empower the bully, so we hid the sting and held back the tears. Or perhaps we fought back with other phrases or with fists, lashing out at the person speaking death to our future. Words can have a deep impact on our lives because words have power.

When my sons were growing up and needed to be disciplined, I was very careful in the language I chose. I would never attack their character but only speak to their actions. "What you are *doing* is bad, but you are not a bad person." Many adults still deal with deep-seated issues of inferiority stemming back to when they were exposed to negative comments.

Why are you such a problem? You'll never amount to anything.

People can continue to act childish long into their adult years because parts of their emotional character never grew past those moments. Indeed, much of the hurtful rhetoric in the world today can be traced to unhealed wounds in those that speak. Hurt people hurt people. Each of us has a choice—even a responsibility—to receive and distribute only words that give life.

Throughout the Gospels, we see people using language to combat the message of faith and hope. In Mark chapter nine, a father brings his convulsing son to Jesus and asks if he can help. The Lord challenges his narrative and exposes his duplicity. "'*If* [I] can [help]?... Everything is possible for the person who believes.'"[1] The father claimed to have faith but used his words to sow unbelief.

On another occasion, a man named Jairus was bringing Jesus to his house to heal his daughter when her situation turned for the worse. The crowd said, "'Your daughter is dead. Why trouble the Teacher any further?'"[2] But Jesus replied that his daughter would live. Which account would Jairus allow to dictate the future of his family? Which words will you allow to have power over your future?

Jesus largely ignored the political winds swirling in his day. Pharisees and Sadducees were prevalent groups, but we have no evidence that Jesus belonged to either of these two major political parties. He was focused on the cross, not the election. As a result, he was verbally attacked by both sides. At one point, the Pharisees declared that Jesus had the power to heal only because he was the servant of the devil.[3] Why would the devil want to bring joy into the lives of the blind and the mute? Indeed, it was the critics that had problems with their vision and vocabulary. Neither of the two political parties were speaking life —they were both part of the problem.

Even secular society understands that words matter. Certain phrases evoke racial tensions, bring division, and inflict insult. People can lose their jobs over a single careless misuse of language. Modern technology has allowed hate speech to be amplified and provided platforms for opinions that divide. In response, online shaming has increased, and individuals and businesses are targeted and become the subjects of boycott and counter-harassment for their divisive words. In some cases, the victims' private information has been posted publicly, and they fear mob violence. When you use the same weapons as your enemy, you become blind to your own role in the problem.

Jesus faced similar issues of hypocrisy from the crowds that followed him.

> "To what, then, can I compare the people of this generation? What are they like? They are like children sitting in the marketplace and calling out to each other: 'We played the flute for you, and you did not dance; we sang a dirge, and you did not cry.'"
>
> — Luke 7:31–32 NIV

To put it another way, no matter what Jesus did, some people would always twist his statements to suit their own worldviews. John the Baptist was mocked for living in isolation, and Jesus was attacked for dining with "sinners." Certain people will always try to tear you down, but it's your decision to give them power or not. You choose whether you will join them and adopt their strategies or will seek life-giving solutions.

The battle over sentiment has reached new levels in modern times. Many people believe that this is a new phenomenon, but words have always had power. The only difference is that today, we make utterances in the absence of relationship. The world lives in a state of fractured connection and reacts from a place of insecurity. One person maligns another from a place of pain and thus creates a new offense in someone else. This creates a cascading series of events until someone breaks that cycle. Christians become believers when they put more faith in the healing power of the cross than the social pressures that surround them.

The tongue is a fire,[4] and it has the power of life and death.[5] Your comments have great potency, regardless of how casual they may seem. When you are confronted by someone using a verbal attack, will you forget your heavenly mission to speak life in response? Will you allow the Lord to heal those places deep in your heart that still have painful scar tissue from old wounds?

Words matter. You matter. The nameless face on the receiving end of your diatribe matters. The world is desperate for someone to break the cycle of the ever-reverberating cacophony of pain. Will you speak the words of life?

23

THE GOSPEL TRUTH (LUKE 4:14–30)

Was Jesus led by the Spirit to go into the desert, or was he led by the Spirit once he entered?[1] Sometimes, seeing the will of God for our lives is easier once we've walked through an open door. As I reflect on this passage in Luke chapter four, I'm struck by the fact that Jesus made that decision to experience what it was like to have very little provision in life. He fasted for forty days, and temptation came to him as the devil tried to alter the course of his earthly ministry.

Jesus left that time of testing and ended up in his hometown of Nazareth, where he stood up and read from the scroll of Isaiah the prophet. This was the thesis statement for his ministry and the essence of the Gospel.

> "The Spirit of the Lord is on me, because he has anointed me to proclaim good news to the poor. He has sent me to proclaim freedom for the prisoners and recovery of sight for the blind, to set the oppressed free, to proclaim the year of the Lord's favor."
>
> — Luke 4:18–19 NIV

Word was already spreading about the unique preaching ability of this man from Nazareth, and the world would soon see dramatic miracles of healing. Those in the synagogue that morning were religious and also believed the Spirit of God was with them. But they had allowed their culture to influence the depth of compassion they were willing to show.

Jesus read from Isaiah chapter sixty-one, but he stopped quoting in a very interesting place. In the very next line, Isaiah speaks about "the day of vengeance of our God."[2] I believe Jesus didn't omit this phrase accidentally, for the cross would satisfy the consequences of sin. Theologians call this *propitiation*, the idea that the wrath of God toward sin has been appeased by the sacrifice being offered. Our message to the world is not one of condemnation but one of compassion.

The good news is that we each can receive

beauty instead of ashes, gladness instead of mourning, and praise instead of despair.[3] We are called to be oaks of righteousness, unmoved by the cultural winds around us. They can rattle our branches, but they cannot shake our roots. We are recipients of these promises, but we are also called to spread the good news.

Many needs all around us threaten to overwhelm us, but the Lord will rebuild the places that have long been devastated, even for many generations. Shame will be replaced with abundant provision, and the inheritance will be joy. For the Lord loves justice, and he desires us to be blessed.[4] Jesus performed miracles because he lived out Isaiah sixty-one, not because he was trying to prove he was the Messiah.

As Jesus spoke in that small synagogue in Nazareth, the listeners already believed they were blessed. They were confident in their place as God's chosen people and eager to hear words that reminded them of these facts. But they became enraged when Jesus brought up two examples in the Scripture of compassion being shown to the Gentiles.

The widow of Zarephath was the Gentile woman who cared for the prophet Elijah during a great drought, and her family was spared from death, while many in Israel died. And Naaman the Syrian was healed of leprosy by Elisha even though he was the commander of the army that fought against Israel. Those were inconvenient historical facts that were difficult for the men in that synagogue to reconcile in their minds. Jesus was trying to get them to understand that true godly compassion extends even to those who may disagree with us. Our mission is to all people, regardless of race, ethnicity, or culture. People matter.

The Jews were so upset about this idea that they physically drove Jesus out of the town and tried to throw him off a cliff, but Jesus was able to continue on his way without harm. He never shied away from disappointing the expectations of religious minds. Miracles were never his focus—his attention was on the people who needed them.

That was the hometown of Jesus. The people had known him from when he was a child, yet he was the one trying to teach them a lesson. The most difficult mission field is found in your own backyard. Will you be a catalyst for change among your own people, or will you let yourself go along with the crowd?

Jesus said, "'Today, this scripture is fulfilled in your hearing.'"[5] The only question remaining is whether it will be fulfilled in you today. You are called to proclaim the reality of the Kingdom of God. Speak life because it's the Gospel truth.

24

SEND SOMEONE ELSE (EXODUS 2–4)

Moses had the call of God on his life. The Hebrews had grown numerous in the land of Egypt, and Pharaoh had ordered the death of thousands of children. As baby Moses floated down the Nile River in a basket, the call of God caused him to be discovered among the reeds by Pharaoh's daughter. Call it luck or call it destiny—Moses was taken from the river and raised in the palace. Some would see it as a privilege to grow up as he did, while others would label it fortuitous, but regardless, Moses was in a position to influence the destiny of his people. None of us has had a choice in where we were born or in what financial or social system we would call home, but what we do with our situation determines our trajectory.

After Moses grew up, he went to where his people were struggling under the bondage of slavery.

Certainly, that wasn't the first time he'd become aware of the injustice being done to the Hebrews. The call of God on Moses was to free his people from the yoke of oppression, and it filled him with passion. One day, Moses saw an Egyptian abusing a Hebrew, and he let passion get the best of him by murdering the Egyptian and hiding his body in the desert sand. The man that would see the finger of God etch basic morality on tablets of stone did himself break what would be the sixth commandment.

Nothing in this story indicates that Moses regretted committing murder, but he soon paid the consequences for his actions. Word spread quickly, and Pharaoh sought to execute him. So Moses escaped once again, this time as an adult. He ended up in the land of Midian and managed to make a decent life for himself. For forty years, Moses tended the flocks on the hills far from Egypt. He was able to ignore his past and move on to greener pastures.

On those lonely and quiet nights, Moses had plenty of opportunities to reflect on how the call of God on his life had been sidetracked by one bad decision. He'd been called to change the destiny of his people but lost his ability to influence change. The person who solves problems with violence has no seat at the mediation table. But as the prophet Habakkuk once said, "If it seems slow in coming, wait patiently, for it will surely take place."[1] The call of God is irrevocable,[2] and Moses could not flee his destiny.

After forty years of isolation, Moses probably thought the sun had set on his dreams. One night, he was on the far side of the desert when he saw a strange sight, a bush that was on fire but wasn't consumed by the flames. Is it possible to have a fire within your heart that does not destroy you? The bush was a living metaphor that beckoned to him. Something stirred deep inside, and he made another decision that would change the rest of his life. Turning aside from his work and his life, he finally took a step toward his destiny.

From within the bush, God identified to Moses who was directing the script: "'I am the God of your father, the God of Abraham, the God of Isaac and the God of Jacob.'"[3] The Lord is the one who sets us on fire, but not for destruction. Moses hid his face, for he was ashamed of many things he'd done. The Lord had heard the cry of the Hebrews and was going to rescue them. He reminded Moses of the plight of his people and tried to awaken the passion within the former prince.

> "So now, go. I am sending you to Pharaoh to bring my people the Israelites out of Egypt."
>
> — Exod 3:10 NIV

Think about the causes that stir your heart, the ones that evoke a strong reaction in your private words or social media posts. What would you do if God appeared to you tonight and asked you to be a part of his solution? Would you volunteer to go, or would you prefer to stay a vocal critic on the sidelines?

Instead of finding strength in the call of God, Moses began listing excuses. *I'm not anyone special. Why should I be the one to go?* I will be with you, and I will give you signs along the way to keep you on track, God told him. *Yeah, but what if they don't listen to me?* You are going in the name of the Lord, not in your own strength. Bring the people the message that God cares for them and their future. *What if the people don't believe in me?* Take what you have, that which you already have in your hands.

God gave Moses the ability to turn his staff into a snake, the power to turn his hand leprous on command, and the means to turn water into blood—but Moses was still scared to go. "'I have never been eloquent... I am slow of speech and tongue.'"[4] The Lord was patient with Moses and reassured him that his words would be given by God—he would be taught what to say. But in the end, Moses had only one reason for objecting to the will of God for his life —he just didn't want to go.

Moses said what most people only think: "'Please send someone else to do it.'"[5] No shortage of armchair quarterbacks and backseat drivers exists. The news media has plenty of time to criticize ideas, because they aren't accountable for any solutions. Being the challenger is easy, but your tone changes when you find yourself the incumbent. Technology amplifies the lethargic criticism from the selfish world of the self-coronated victim. If these words offend you, then you might be spending too much time on the sidelines and not enough time on the field. "'The harvest is plentiful, but the workers are few,'"[6] but all too often, a small percentage of the church does the majority of the work.

Instead of asking ourselves why the world has so many problems, maybe we should be asking why more people aren't actively working toward solutions. Too many people make the Moses mistake and believe that passion is enough. They resort to violence and hatred, taking instead of giving and loving. Instead of posting another social media rant, maybe the solution involves action instead of talking.

The Lord's anger burned against Moses. That was his chance to finally respond to the injustice being done to his people, but the man who had grown accustomed to staying far from the problems had no shortage of excuses. However, God called his brother Aaron to serve alongside Moses, and together, they pried the entire race of Hebrews from the land of bondage.

That is not to say the task wasn't difficult. God brought the Israelites out of Egypt, but removing bondage from the hearts of the people took another forty years. Countless challenges materialized along the way to the Promised Land, just as you will face struggles in your life. But the journey toward freedom starts with the simple decision to go. Will your life be marked by complaints and criticism of those that are doing the work, or will you join them and cultivate lasting solutions? Are you willing to be quiet long enough to hear what solutions the Lord has in mind? Are you willing to go, or will you ask the Lord to send someone else?

25

THE OPPORTUNITY TO COMPLAIN (MARK 6:30–44)

Jesus's ministry was thriving, and large crowds were following him as he traveled the countryside, and the apostles were also teaching and seeing miracles firsthand. They were all tired and needed a change of pace, so Jesus said, "'Come with me by yourselves to a quiet place and get some rest.'"[1]

We are surrounded by technology that makes life easier and more comfortable, yet stress and anxiety characterize our lives. We are busy with many tasks, but finding time for things that truly matter is increasingly difficult. If ever there was a time that we needed a break, it's now.

When we deliberately press the pause button, it allows us to reflect on the decisions we're making and the directions our lives are going. Quiet has a way of calming the nerves, allowing us to sort through the demands being placed upon us. This is where we develop the strength necessary to weather the storms of life because, when an emergency comes, we won't have time to prepare.

Jesus and his disciples got into a boat and went to a solitary place, but when they arrived, they found the crowd had traveled ahead of them. They were seeking rest but couldn't escape the pressure of the ministry. Groups of sick and desperate souls would've been there, longing for miracles, along with many skeptics looking for a way to have them arrested—rich and poor, seekers and cynics, needy and selfish people as far as the eye could see. The crowd wasn't thinking about the work-life balance of the apostles as they clamored for more time with the traveling teacher.

The disciples came to Jesus and complained, "'This is a remote place, and it's already getting late. Send the crowds away so they can go to the nearby farms and villages and buy something to eat.'"[2] Like celebrities after a concert, they were done performing, and these people didn't have a backstage pass. The apostles needed a break, and the crowd just wouldn't go away. But every challenge you face presents a choice. Will you allow creativity to flow, or will you complain?

Every invention ever created was a solution to a problem. Someone let the pain of a predicament motivate them to resolve an obstacle that others could not overcome. From indoor plumbing to automobiles, inventors were just people that saw headaches as opportunities. They stand out as unique because most people wait for someone else to do all the work.

Ironically, the believers were guilty of the same mistake as the crowds—they wanted Jesus to solve their problems. But that is not how you train students. If you are going to be an apprentice, you need to learn the tools of the trade. Jesus said, "'You give them something to eat.'"[3]

Have you ever taken an academic exam in which you were confused about one of the questions? Perhaps you went for clarification to the instructor, who gave you a clue but not the complete answer. The whole point of the exam was to test your understanding and see if you could do the work. Jesus was conducting a pop quiz, and he wanted to see how his pupils would respond.

> "That would take more than half a year's wages! Are we to go and spend that much on bread and give it to them to eat?"
>
> — Mark 6:37 NIV

Interestingly, they apparently had enough

money to solve the problem that way but struggled with the cost of meeting the need. Judas Iscariot wasn't the only one that liked a healthy supply of coins in the money bag.[4]

Money has an interesting hold upon us—worthless metal and paper, mere tokens that represent some level of effort or value we have stored. You cannot take it with you, but entire lives are spent pursuing it. If you are focused merely on earthly events, then money might be of value, but heavenly solutions have a different source.

I've noticed some people have trouble donating finances, while others have difficulty giving their time, but both are rooted in selfishness. It reveals a belief that a resource is scarce and needs to be protected. But Jesus challenged his followers to invest both their time and wealth in the only asset that produces consistent returns.

He asked the disciples to inventory their food supply, which was scarcely enough for the ministry team, let alone five thousand men, women, and children. Maybe they were hangry because they didn't have enough food for themselves, for we learn in John's Gospel that the five loaves of bread and two fish were given by a young boy.[5] The wisdom of a child was not encumbered by what adults believed was impossible. He entrusted his resources to the Lord and watched them multiply.

This is not an easy lesson, and just two chapters

later, an identical situation arises.[6] Another large crowd had gathered, and the people were without food. Jesus asked his followers what they should do, and they failed the test again. This time, the crowd was smaller—only four thousand men. Had they really forgotten the miracle so quickly? Deliberate and daily effort to use Kingdom thinking is needed as we view the problems in society.

Helping people is not a hobby or something to be done when we have extra time. We should not be surprised when impossible needs are thrust into our lives because we are the ones that supposedly hold the solution. Government programs can be extremely helpful in meeting certain community needs, but that does not exempt believers from bringing meaningful change. Don't let donating money be your excuse for not giving your time. True disciples do not complain from the sidelines—they get personally involved.

26

WHO DO YOU THINK YOU ARE? (JOHN 8:12–59)

Jesus spent the majority of his ministry trying to stretch the minds and faith of his listeners. Heaven had come down to earth, but people struggled to comprehend the magnitude of the differences between the two. The earthly governments and culture had become so diametrically opposed to the Kingdom of Heaven that they didn't recognize the arrival of the Messiah.[1] Many tense exchanges occurred as Jesus presented a better point of view, because humans have a tendency to dislike being told what to do.

Our brains are wired to process vast amounts of information in a very short amount of time. We create mental filters based on previous data in an attempt to adjust to the ever-changing environment. This is a useful adaptation skill in the animal kingdom, but it can reinforce incorrect thinking that prevents you from being open to new concepts that might contradict what you already hold to be true.

Confirmation bias is the tendency to process and analyze information in such a way that it supports one's preexisting ideas and convictions.[2] Ironically, the very phrase has been used as a weapon to invalidate the ideas of others and label them as closed-minded, but we all have biases. Every experience changes how you will react to a new situation. A child that is attacked by a dog will struggle with embracing one as a pet later in life. Every painful moment has a trigger that can affect how we deal with new people and situations. Those seeking healing will do their best to overcome the past and move on, but we would be remiss to think any of us operate free from prejudice.

One day, Jesus was teaching in the temple area when the religious leaders brought a woman who'd been caught in the act of adultery. The teachers of the Law wanted her to be stoned because that was their understanding of justice. Jesus tried to get them to recognize that they had been unfaithful to the Lord their God, but their minds did not have room. They were fully convinced that her sin was much larger than theirs.

Jesus went on to speak about his father in heaven, but his critics thought he was describing his earthly lineage. He was not from this world and warned them that they were enslaved by sin and needed to be emancipated.

> "We are Abraham's descendants and have never been slaves of anyone. How can you say that we shall be set free?"
>
> —John 8:33 NIV

They were offended by the truth and couldn't see past their own misunderstandings. They were no longer in Egypt, but they certainly weren't free from Rome. "'Abraham is our father,'" they answered, but Jesus disagreed. "'If you were Abraham's children... then you would do what Abraham did.'"[3] Now the debate was on. They were being called illegitimate children as their credentials were being challenged. This escalated their assertions as they claimed to be children of God, the very concept they'd failed to understand when the debate began.

We become hypocrites when we expect more from others than we are willing to give. Narcissists are those who have an inflated sense of self-importance and a constant need for attention. They had dismissed Jesus when he claimed God as his father but then used that very argument for their own self-legitimacy. We don't let anyone tell us we're wrong, and we're sure to correct them when they try. We love rules except when they get applied to us because we're convinced we are already correct.

The chief priests returned the perceived insults, making a racist slur and declaring him to be possessed by a demon,[4] but Jesus refused to bend the truth to fit into their biases. They weren't following Abraham's example, and they had created a god in their own image—one that stayed in the box where he belonged. Jesus shattered all their pretenses, and their religious minds exploded at the gall of this self-declared teacher. "'Who do you think you are?'" they asked.[5] "'Very truly I tell you,' Jesus answered, 'before Abraham was born, I am.'"[6] They were not able to accept his words, for they contradicted everything they held to be true. They picked up stones to kill him, but Jesus slipped away into the crowds.

I used to enjoy Sudoku puzzles. These simple but complex riddles contain eighty-one squares divided into nine groupings, each arranged like a tic-tac-toe board. The object is to place the numbers one through nine into each of the locations, such that the same number does not appear more than once in any row, column, or subgrouping. How many correct numerical positions the puzzle creator provides at the beginning determines the relative difficulty of the challenge.

At first, the mathematical logic and the process of elimination appealed to my analytical mind and gave me a sense of accomplishment when I solved them. But I recall spending one entire Sunday afternoon juggling the matrix of options in my mind as I filled in the squares with my pencil. (This was back before computers and apps assisted you in undoing your decisions.)

As the afternoon progressed, I gradually reached the end of my task and had two squares left. I tried placing the two remaining digits into each of the locations and realized the move was incorrect. I switched the numbers, and much to my surprise, that move was also invalid. This meant that one of my previous selections had led me to a dead end. As I retraced a preceding choice, that again yielded only mistaken results. I tried to remember past options and quickly realized I was too late. Somewhere along the way, I had made a bad assumption and now couldn't unravel the mistake. For each move I'd made, I was firmly convinced I was right, but I couldn't argue with the end result. I had completely wasted my entire afternoon and felt like a total failure.

Life is like a Sudoku puzzle. We try our best to make good choices, and each new decision is based, in part, on previous assumptions. But what if our suppositions prove to be incorrect? What if we live the majority of our lives, only to realize one of the foundational pillars we've used for support is just wrong? That is the cost of bias.

The lens by which you view the world will taint your impressions. All of us want to live in a place where things make sense. We don't like it when bad things happen to good people, and we get anxious when encountering ideas that disrupt our worldviews. Life can seem like a mystery, and we need the pieces to fall into place. Very mature people are able to take a step back and weigh the mores that have formed their views and shaped their beliefs. Culture gives us meaning, and a town can become a community as neighbors seem like family, but Jesus challenges believers to align their thoughts with the Kingdom of Heaven.

If you think about it, every parable and lesson that Jesus gave challenged the assumptions of how we view the world. The Gospel requires us to rise above our cultural doctrines and examine how our faith has been tainted by our experiences. Jesus challenges us to acknowledge the bias contained in every earthly culture and answer the question, "Who do you think you are?"

27

INFINITE BLESSINGS (LUKE 15:11–32)

In biblical times, complex inheritance laws dictated how the wealth of a family passed to the next generation. The eldest son would receive a double portion, twice what the other sons would inherit.[1] If no male children had been born, the estate would be divided among the daughters.[2] Widows were required to remarry within the bloodline in order to keep the endowment within the family, and the nearest male relative was obligated to redeem the potentially tragic situation when the patriarch of a family died.[3] Jesus used this cultural backdrop as the context of his story about selfishness and greed.

"'There was a man who had two sons.'"[4] Both of them would someday share in the estate of their father, but the younger son grew inpatient. He broke the customs of his day and demanded his share while his father was still alive. To make matters worse, he sold the inheritance for cash so that he could engage in wild living. Family protocol was being violated in so many ways in this story that Jesus was obviously trying to anger his listeners. This was a gross injustice being perpetrated by the younger son, so offensive that such an arrangement might never have actually been possible under the Jewish Law.

The younger son was the personification of selfish entitlement. Family inheritances had been strictly guarded since the time of Joshua, but the younger son demanded what he did not honor and sold it as something that had no value. He disrespected the generational labor of his ancestors and had no respect for his family name. Only when he lost everything did he finally come to his senses. He returned to his homeland starving and humiliated.

How should society treat people that have hit rock bottom due to their own bad decisions? Do any consequences exist for someone who has squandered resources in a selfish lifestyle? Jesus was prodding his listeners. Many of them probably knew someone that had done something similar. Maybe you have a friend or family member who has challenged the extent of your devotion. Do they need to learn the valuable lesson of tough love or feel the warm embrace of compassion and empathy?

> But while he was still a long way off, his father saw him and was filled with compassion for him; he ran to his son, threw his arms around him and kissed him.
>
> — Luke 15:20 NIV

The father in this story saw the prodigal son while he was still a distance away. He ran to him and helped him return home. He covered his son's shame with the best robe and gave him sandals for his wandering feet. A ring was put on his finger to remind him that true inheritance is not found in worldly wealth and that the only way to leave the family of God is to choose to no longer be a part of it —home is where you are celebrated and not just tolerated.[5]

A party began, and the fattened calf was prepared. The father was always willing to give his best to his sons—they didn't need to make demands of him. The younger son was learning what true love felt like. This is the same lesson a Christian can learn when the weight of their sin is lifted as they gaze upon the cross. We didn't deserve to be called children of God, but the grace of the Lord overwhelmed us anyway.

When the eldest son returned from the fields, he

heard the sound of music and dancing. Like many of us, he became offended at forgiveness being given to someone that has committed a transgression. He refused to celebrate the safe return of his brother, indignant at the long list of fraternal offenses.

He had worked for his father his entire life and felt he was never celebrated in this same manner. He believed the way to his father's heart was to earn his love through actions. One third of the family inheritance had been lost, and the thief was not being held accountable. Now, a portion of his future inheritance was being used to throw a party for his wayward brother. It's one thing when someone loses their own money but quite another when they take yours.

The economies of this world are often subject to a zero-sum game, where one person's win is another's loss.[6] If a government wants to develop a program to help people in need, they must raise the money by taking it from those that have plenty. How you see this redistribution of wealth depends on which side of the equation you are on. For instance, I have noticed that many such programs are popular as long as the voters are convinced that someone else will bear the financial burden. We all enjoy a free lunch because we aren't ending up with the bill.

Did the older brother in this story feel like he was paying for his brother's party? Did he resent his father bailing out his brother by using the remaining family resources? Was he committing the same selfish error as his younger brother by subtly claiming his inheritance before his father died?

The Kingdom of God doesn't operate in the same manner as earthly kingdoms. Our heavenly father doesn't need to take something away from one person in order to bless another. Nobody needs to play the zero-sum game when we have access to infinite blessings. However, your heart will remain conflicted between the two realms as long as you view inheritance as a transfer of earthly wealth.

Jesus constantly challenged his followers to change their thinking. He violated the laws of physics when he walked upon the water[7] and kept a money bag for ministry expenses even though he could pull coins from the mouth of a fish.[8] He bent the principles of science with every miracle he performed. The overall theme of each lesson was that the Kingdom of God is not like the kingdom of earth. You don't need to be stingy with the blessings you have received because the Lord is your source, and his supply is limitless. Citizens of heaven need to recognize the selfish attitude that wants to both keep what you have received and demand that others give you what you did not earn.

I think Jesus loved to tell parables because he knew we listen better when someone provides a story rather than a lecture. They present noncontroversial ways to learn lessons because the listeners get to choose the characters to which they will relate. Do you see yourself in the actions of the younger son, feeling the sting of bad decisions and desperation for mercy? Do you expect the father and the older brother to replace what you lost? Or are you a bit like the eldest son, unwilling to see past an offense of another and feeling that you have earned your blessings with hard work and perseverance?

We are children of God. The father is both patient and persistent, wanting the best for each of us. Godly blessings cannot be received until we recognize the source of heaven's bounty. The father wants to pass on the inheritance, and his supply is infinite.

28

DON'T BLAME ME (GENESIS 3)

Since the dawn of time, people have been blaming others for negative situations, but the original design was harmony. In the book of Genesis, we see how the Lord God placed a man and a woman in the very center of all he'd created. They were united, one literally taken from the essence of the other. Working as a team, they cared for all the other living things as they tended the garden. They walked and talked with God, and their home was the definition of paradise.

The couple faced only one limitation. They were allowed to eat of all the trees in the garden except for the one in the middle. The Tree of the Knowledge of Good and Evil bore the one fruit they were not created to experience. That one bad decision sent the world tumbling down a path that led to self-destruction and eons of pain. But before all that took place, a single voice of doubt floated in the morning mist.

> "Did God really say, 'You must not eat from any tree in the garden?'"
>
> — Gen 3:1 NIV

This has become a timeless question among centuries of believers who have wrestled with their conscience as they attempted to live out their faith. What did God actually say? Does the Lord of the universe have an opinion on the moral questions that challenge your culture? Some give license to sin, while others add layers of legalism that were never intended, but both have become like Eve as she added to the Lord's instructions. "The woman said to the serpent, 'We may eat fruit from the trees in the garden, but God did say, "You must not eat fruit from the tree that is in the middle of the garden, and *you must not touch it*, or you will die."'"[1]

The man and the woman both ate of the fruit, and the rest of the Bible tells the consequences of their hasty decision. They should've ignored the voice of the serpent and trusted in their Lord, but now their offspring would live among increasing evil and violence.

The couple heard the Lord walking in the cool of the day and felt shame for the first time, hiding themselves from the one who sees into our hearts. But the Lord God knew they'd become lost as he called to them, "'Where are you?'"[2] Every adult that has ever stood in front of a child with crumbs on their face knows the rest of this story. *"The cookie jar is empty, but it's not my fault."*

"Where are you?"

— Gen 3:9 NIV

Adam accuses Eve, and she blames the serpent, but all three of them knew the rules. The man was standing next to his wife when she was discussing what the Lord had said. They were partners, yet he let his team down. In his silence, he abdicated his responsibility to lead and sabotaged the trajectory of his family line. She didn't need to make that decision alone and failed to leverage the wisdom of her husband. In her desire for knowledge, she allowed her ignorance to override common sense, opening the door for evil to enter their world. Plenty of mistakes were made by everyone, but none were owned. Seeing the damage now is easy, but seldom does anyone admit to wrongdoing. We all have crumbs on our faces, and we need to stop acting like children.

Blaming other people creates an atmosphere of division that perpetuates discord and prevents cooperation. How were Adam and Eve supposed to work together going forward if they couldn't be honest about their roles in "Garden-gate"?[3] When their son Cain murdered his brother Abel on a whim, we see no regret in the attitude of his parents because they had created a blame culture. What might have been different if the couple had confessed their mistakes to one another and worked to prevent additional fractures?

Many of the problems in the modern world could arguably be traced to the issue of broken relationships. Human beings are inherently tribal,[4] so we tend to gather in homogeneous groups. We create boundaries based on gender and race, economics and business, religion and politics. We develop marketing campaigns to ensure certain groups are marginalized by using terms like anti, hater, and closed-minded. We are convinced that problems could be solved if not for the extremists, the radicals, and the zealots. Conservatives fear the erosion of the moral fabric of society while liberals bemoan the inequity of western culture. Passions are flying high as the left battles the right for the power to coerce. We see the sins of the other groups so clearly that we justify our own attitudes and behavior.[5] From our self-coronated seats of judgement, we absolve ourselves by declaring, "It's not my fault."

What would happen if you stopped blaming someone long enough to listen to what they had to say? What are their fears and doubts? What experiences have they had in life that have influenced them to rally to the causes they choose? The believer is called to unclench their fists and use their hands to embrace, to touch, and to guide.

Some people use words like *privilege* and *entitlement* to bludgeon their listeners with their worldviews and forfeit any chance of working toward a common solution. This doesn't mean that the issues of inequity aren't real or shouldn't be discussed, but if our goal is to solve the problem, should we alienate our potential advocates? The Bible reminds us that our words are powerful.[6] For the believer, personal responsibility invites you not to blame another group of people for the situation in which you find yourself. It means coming to terms with your role in any given problem and being mature enough to admit it without *requiring* other people to confess their role in a situation. What you do with what the Lord has placed in your hands reveals how deeply the cross has impacted your life.[7]

The Gospel is a simple message of hope. A tiny baby born into humble circumstances destroyed the barrier between kings and shepherds, men and women, indeed all who would seek to create any wall of division. Believers have tasted the mercy of the cross and no longer play the blame game. We don't let other voices deceive us into viewing our differences as divisions. Let's use all that the Lord has freely given to us—our words and our resources—to show the world the love that is in our hearts.

29

DRY BONES (EZEKIEL 37)

I have always enjoyed hiking in the mountains. Something about the struggle up the path is very fulfilling and makes the view from the top seem more rewarding. The anticipation builds as the tree cover thins at higher elevations, allowing increased sunlight to fall upon your face. With aching muscles, we press on and encourage those that are with us, reminding them that the goal of the summit must be close. We find new strength as the pitch of the trail levels off, leading toward the large rocks guarding the peak. We feel the unbridled wind as it forces us to lean into our pace and forms goosebumps on our skin, instantly cooling our sweat-stained clothing as we come to rest. We scan the horizon, seeing for hundreds of miles in all directions. All the pain of getting to this point is forgotten or worn as a badge of honor. We allow smiles to creep across our faces as we come to the realization that the challenge was worth it.

The Prophet Ezekiel was standing in a valley, that place between the high points in life. That he was there was no accident, for the Lord had brought him to that point. As he looked around, he saw dry bones covering the surface of the earth, and the voice of the Lord asked him a simple question.

> "Son of man, can these bones live?"
>
> — Ezek 37:3 NIV

We all find ourselves in valleys at some point, and these bones serve as a reminder that not everyone makes it out alive. We tend to seek the pinnacle moments, but in order to get to the mountaintop, you need to go through the valley. In the familiar words of Psalm twenty-three, "[T]hough I walk through the valley of the shadow of death, I will fear no evil; For You are with me; Your rod and Your staff, they comfort me."[1] The valley is something we go *through*, but we are not meant to live there.

Ezekiel was staring at the evidence that people can get stuck in a moment in time, becoming dry and losing their will to proceed. Our dreams regarding our future become clouded by the difficulty of the daily struggle. In those pivotal moments, we are faced with a decision as to which destiny we will choose. Will your future be characterized by life or death, by failure or triumph?

Ezekiel was a prophet, but his calling was not as unique as you might think. We are all called to speak to our present situation and command it to come into alignment with our preferred future. For our God is the one "who gives life to the dead and calls into existence the things that do not exist."[2]

Can these bones live? The Prophet replied, "'Sovereign Lord, you alone know.'"[3] Indeed, the Lord is the giver of life,[4] the one who knows the end from the beginning,[5] but that was not the question. Do we believe what the Lord has already said? Are we brave enough to stand in the gap[6] and prophesy life in the middle of what seems like hopelessness?

The Lord gave Ezekiel the words to say and showed him the will of God: Speak to the bones and command them to listen. Fresh air will come upon them, and newfound strength will raise them to new life. Then they will know that I am the Lord.

Ezekiel did as he was instructed, and even as he was still speaking, he heard a noise. A rattling sound emerged from the valley floor as bones came together. God brought order to the chaos,[7] and the ravine suddenly contained a vast army of lifeless forms, for they had no breath.

What an amazing sight it must have been to see

soldiers formed out of the dust of the ground but not rising to their full stature. Why was the miracle not complete? Why had they come so far, only to fail at the moment of birth? It reminds me of how Elijah required three attempts to raise the widow's son from the dead[8] and how Jesus applied mud twice to the blind man's eyes near the village of Bethsaida.[9] When you don't see the results for which you had hoped, will you give up or doubt the Lord that led you there? The consistent embrace of resistance is what gives a body builder their muscles.

In that moment of potential setback, the voice of the sovereign Lord penetrated the doubt in his mind: Speak to the breath. Breathe into those who lie slain and command them to live. Do not allow the limitations of the doubters to persuade you into settling for less than the full blessing of God. Ezekiel spoke, and a mighty army rose to life.

This vision was a metaphor for Ezekiel and for modern believers—for all those who have ever said, "Our bones are dried up, and our hope has perished. We are completely finished."[10] Your life on earth can rob you of your joy and make you feel like a failure, but when the pressure of anxiety weighs heavy on your shoulders and the problems seem to outnumber the solutions—when you are tempted to quit or too tired to try—that is when you need to remember this story. Newness of life is just a breath away.

I have always enjoyed hiking in the mountains,

but I have never lived on one. After enjoying the clear vision from the top, I have descended to lower elevations. Moses had to come down from Mount Sinai to help lead the people.[11] Peter wanted to pitch a tent and stay on the Mount of Transfiguration,[12] but Jesus knew that they needed to return to the ministry. We enjoy the mountaintops, but we are called to the valleys.

The world is full of problems because that's where people live. Dry bones exist in every society, needs that require someone to make a stand. Prophesy to the dry bones in your community and tell them they do not need to quit. Prophesy to your own heart because your words have power. Speak life, and let's believe together that the army of the Lord will rise to fulfill their destiny.

30

WHAT DO YOU HAVE LEFT? (MARK 12:41–44, LUKE 21:1–4)

You can tell a lot about someone's faith by looking at their bank or credit card statement because it reveals the truth about how you really live your life. It's easy to raise your voice with the choir but much harder to donate your time and money to fix the church building. In fact, church-giving percentages are lower today than they were during the Great Depression.[1] The very topic of tithing is considered by many to be heresy or an outdated concept preached by manipulative preachers. But the Bible has always reminded us that "where your treasure is, there your heart will be also."[2]

While he was on earth, Jesus had a lot to say about the financial system the world was using. In fact, the Bible has over two thousand verses that deal with money and possessions.[3] Jesus brought up the topic of provision in many of his parables because it exposed the intentions of the hearts he was trying to touch. Money should never be our goal, but it can become an obstacle.

The day after the Triumphal Entry, Jesus went to the temple and was enraged by the extortion taking place. His people had turned the house of God into a marketplace and were getting rich from the pilgrims coming to the city to worship God. He was so mad that he made a whip out of cords to drive the livestock from the Temple area, chasing everyone away from their places, turning over their tables and spilling their ill-gained profits on the ground.[4] Very clearly, Jesus has an opinion on how we make and spend our money.

I've lived most of my life in North America and have noticed that the overwhelming majority of people believe they are in the middle class.[5] When politicians talk about "taxing the rich," most people agree because they don't believe they are the target. But in fact, Western nations now hold almost all the world's wealth[6] despite many long-standing social issues that can be traced to income inequality within their borders. There is a great dichotomy between the haves and the have-nots, and the gap is increasing.[7]

An economy can be defined as a system of exchanging value within a community. We use the term "money" as the quantification of value, and it personifies what our culture esteems. However, the

Kingdom of God is run by an entirely different system. This is perhaps why Jesus used parables. The Kingdom of God is so vastly different from any kingdom on earth that our minds struggle to comprehend it.

One day, Jesus was sitting and watching the place where donations were given at the temple. Many rich people came and threw in great sums, making a commotion and enjoying being the praised benefactors. The priests needed the large donations and made sure the donors felt appreciated. But Jesus was not impressed. When a poor widow came forward, she was invisible to all earthly eyes, for she only dropped in a paltry amount, less than a penny. That was all she had to live on, and it was a huge sacrifice for her to make. Jesus was so overwhelmed that he instantly beckoned his disciples so that they could learn a very important truth. The woman had given more to the Kingdom of God than all the combined gifts from the rich. Though she wasn't publicly congratulated for her sacrificial giving, Jesus proclaimed that her gift was more valuable than all the rest.

> Calling his disciples to him, Jesus said, "Truly I tell you, this poor widow has put more into the treasury than all the others. They all gave out of their wealth; but she, out of her

> poverty, put in everything—all she had to live on."
>
> — Mark 12:41–44 NIV

A trend has been growing among the billionaires of the world, to take the Giving Pledge, agreeing to donate half of their wealth to charity at or before the time of their death.[8] Many have even agreed to give ninety-nine percent of their estate. This sizable amount will be a lifeline to many struggling charities around the globe, and it represents an enormous quantity of money. But Jesus said that the gift of a penny from the hand of a widow was more valuable than all the opulent gifts of the magnates. His statement is as controversial in our day as it was two thousand years ago. The Son of God would look at these wealthy billionaires and basically say, "So what?" In the economy of heaven, it's not how much you give but how much you have left that determines your generosity.

Don't misunderstand me—I commend those taking the Giving Pledge, for they are in the minority. Most of us give very little[9] and still make sure we tell our friends if we pay for someone's coffee in the drive-through at Starbucks. I chuckle when people "pay it forward" by then paying for the person next in line, because if you think about it, only the person that started the chain really did anything.

I heard a story once about a village in Mexico that contained some of the happiest people on earth. A strong family connection and a culture of honor existed in the community. They considered themselves rich because they had everything they needed. One day, a group of people arrived from north of the border and were struck by the sincerity they witnessed. They felt compelled to help the village toward a greater economic situation. But when the people in the village saw what they didn't have, they became depressed. Their perspective changed, and now they believed themselves to be poor. What was viewed by some as a financial problem became a mental health issue.

The widow in our story was dirt poor and remained in poverty after she finished giving her offering. We want the story to end with her coming into great wealth as her generosity is multiplied. That does sometimes happen, but it just isn't the story for billions of people across the planet. It seems unfair, and we struggle to make sense of a God that would allow so much inequity. But the truth for a believer is that wealth is not measured in euros or dollar bills—true riches are available to everyone who comes to the foot of the cross.

The litmus test for any disciple is the grip we keep on what we find in our hands, for we are stewards of what the Lord has entrusted to us. Inequity will always be among us until the issue of sin and selfishness is fully in the rearview mirror, but that doesn't mean we should resign ourselves to being a part of the problem. The true believer is a conduit of blessing for the Lord to impact the hearts of needy world.

What do you have left? For some, addressing this question will mean increased financial generosity, and for others, it will involve a greater investment of time. The key point is that each of us must look inward and examine what we have been holding back for ourselves.

31

COUNT ME IN (2 SAM 24)

King David reigned in Jerusalem during the height of the Jewish nation, when Israel and Judah were united as a single empire. In his humble beginnings as a shepherd, he played his harp under the stars when he wasn't fighting off apex predators while guarding the flock.[1] He was a man after God's own heart and was anointed by the prophet Samuel to succeed King Saul.[2] Although he was a monarch, perhaps you can relate to the unending family drama and constant cycle of highs and lows. From the defeat of Goliath to the adultery with Bathsheba, David's life was filled with ups and downs.

Toward the end of his life, as he was preparing to hand the kingdom over to his son Solomon, he decided to take a census. Rather than trusting in the Lord's strength to protect the nation from its enemies, David instructed his commander Joab to count the men available for battle. Joab reluctantly obeyed the instruction, and one million three hundred thousand soldiers were identified in the land.

The Lord had done miracles through David and his band of three hundred mighty men, but now the king's legacy faltered. Those men had come to him at the lowest point in his life, when he was being hunted by King Saul. They were an eclectic group of misfits that had nothing but their passion, men whom God had used to accomplish amazing things. David didn't need a human army because the Lord makes us mighty, not personality traits or learned skills.

It has become popular to do case studies on famous people in an attempt to glean the formulas for their success. We want to believe in magic spells, simple methods for gaining favorable outcomes, because we insist upon shortcuts to prosperity and blessing. But as any successful investor understands, the compounding results of good decisions over a long period of time are what change the bottom line. What you accomplish in life isn't what makes you successful, but who you become along the way.

David was confronted by the Lord for his actions and given the choice to pick the consequence: either three years of famine, three years of fleeing from his enemies, or three days of plague. David was in deep distress as the impact of his mistake weighed heavy on his heart. He had spent years hiding in caves and was intimately familiar with the ravages of war, so only one option was palatable. He said, "'Let us fall into the hands of the Lord, for his mercy is great; but do not let me fall into human hands.'"[3]

Seventy thousand people died in the next two days as the virus spread throughout the nation. The disease had reached the home of a man named Araunah the Jebusite when the Lord commanded it to stop. David took full responsibility for his actions.

> "These people are like sheep with me as their shepherd. I have sinned terribly, but they have done nothing wrong. Please, punish me and my family instead of them!"
>
> — 2 Sam 24:17 CEV

Admitting personal responsibility does not come easy to our society. Many people expect mercy for themselves while demanding justice for others. We are convinced we're the victims and should not have to face the repercussions of our choices. But leadership is not achieved by following the crowd, nor is success measured by opinion polls. The Lord had chosen David precisely because of his character and not his charisma.

David was led by God to pay a visit to the location where the plague had ceased in order to build an altar to the Lord. He offered to purchase the land, but Araunah wanted to give him the threshing floor, along with the oxen required for the sacrifice. David was entitled to take whatever was necessary, and that was his privilege as the king, but he refused.

> "No, but I will buy it from you for a price. I will not offer burnt offerings to the LORD my God that cost me nothing."
>
> — 2 Sam 24:24 ESV

In biblical days, the people would harvest grain and place it on a hard surface called a threshing floor. There it would be crushed and ground together, allowing the grain to be freed from the stalks. Workers would throw it into the air by hand or with a winnowing fork, allowing the breeze to blow the lighter chaff away as the heavier grain fell to the ground. Picking a location where the power of the wind would make the work easier was essential, so the altar was being built in a valuable location.

Although today's farmers use machines to harvest and prepare grain, God is still in the business of sifting his people. Making the valuable parts available for use requires pressure upon our lives. You may feel like you're being crushed and exposed when, in fact, you're being trained. Opposition and obstacles are simply opportunities for increased harvest. Leaders are not born—they are forged. These men and women have allowed themselves to be examined like wheat is winnowed as the wind of the Holy Spirit purifies their souls. We cannot lament what is lost in the process, for it was just worthless chaff that needed to be removed.

As technology allowed this procedure to be moved into an outbuilding, farmers attached a board to the bottom of each doorway so that the grain would not spill out of the barn. This panel became known as the "threshold," for it was the border between the abrasive process of threshing and the purifying action of winnowing by the wind. It's the metaphorical decision point that separates your current situation from the promise of your future. This indoor method also allowed grain to be processed during the winter season, free from the natural elements. Indeed, the work of the Holy Spirit seems more intense in the harder seasons of life. The foundation for the spring is laid when it seems like all life has disappeared. The wind of the Spirit is blowing, and you must decide to step through the door.

David's life was full of moments when the Lord was sifting his heart for all to read, and he was no stranger to painful memories. He was rejected by his family[4] and pursued by countless enemies. His sons were rebels,[5] rapists,[6] and murderers.[7] His boss was fixated on killing him, and his best friend died in battle.[8] He violated many of the Ten Commandments, including the ones forbidding adultery and murder.[9] Life had exacted a high payment from the shepherd boy, but in spite of all of that, he stood at the end of his life and declared, "'I will not make an offering to the Lord that costs me nothing.'"[10]

The Lord never promised you that life on earth would be easy. Committing our lives to the Lord can never be done with preconditions or prenuptial agreements. Christianity is a lifelong journey during which we discover that the cross is not a Christmas tree. The only thing underneath is the life we surrender. From that point on, we daily recommit to being sifted and processed, crushed and winnowed. Believers cannot take their own census, relying on the things of this world to bring what only the Lord can provide. We will know we have become successful when we can look back at life and see his fingerprints at every stage of our journey and declare, "I wouldn't change a thing." As I think about the tremendous cost, I can honestly say, "Count me in."

CLAIM YOUR FREE BOOK

Sign up for the mailing list to receive a free copy of "Think About Your Peace." You'll also receive news about upcoming books and thoughts from the author.

http://www.JWClarkAuthor.com

If you enjoyed this book, would you take a moment to leave a review on Amazon, Bookbub, and Goodreads, or the retailer where you purchased this book?

THINK ABOUT CHRISTMAS

A PREVIEW OF BOOK #3 IN THE "THINK ABOUT" SERIES

Christmas is my favorite holiday. I love driving down residential streets and seeing the lights adorning the houses. Each day additional decorations are displayed as the holiday momentum builds. People seem to have a little more bounce in their step and kindness seems more prevalent than the rest of the year. The stress around purchasing gifts or cleaning the house for the arrival of guests is mitigated by the desire within believers to celebrate the arrival of the Messiah.

For many people, Christmas is not a religious holiday and the stores focus on secular music but the choruses of the faith can still be heard. "Joy to the world, the Lord has come. Let earth receive her king." Two thousand years ago, a baby was born that would literally restart the calendar, but his own did not receive him. "'I am the light of the world. Whoever follows me will never walk in darkness, but will have the light of life.'"

As a child, I was anxious for Christmas morning. My parents would take my sister and me to church where my anticipation grew exponentially as the advent season progressed. The minister would light one of the candles each week as he highlighted different aspects of the nativity story: The angel Gabriel appearing to Mary and the ensuing journey to Bethlehem, the stable, the shepherds and the wisemen. The traditional Christmas hymns still fill me with wonderful childhood recollections to this day. But not all memories at Christmas are filled with joy.

When I was ten years old, I remember that my father didn't join us for the Christmas Eve service. He and my mother were getting divorced and our family was adjusting as many families do. In the middle of one of the hymns, I noticed both my mother and sister were crying and I did not know why. My sister subtly motioned to the back of the church where I saw my father standing alone with tears streaming down his face. The symbolism of the moment is still poignant in my mind as I remember turning back toward the front of the church to dry my own eyes. When I glanced back a moment later, he was gone. I remember wishing that he would sit with us, if only for that one night.

The emotional grip of that memory is still strong in my heart. Decades have passed and I have a fantastic relationship with both my parents but that memory is not something that I will ever forget though the years have changed the way I interpret it. Christmas is my favorite holiday, but, like many people, not all my memories are happy ones.

The focus on family at Christmas causes all types of life experience to bubble to the surface. Some people have holes in their heart caused by losing a loved one, robbing them of Christmas memories never created. Others spend the holiday alone in empty homes devoid of decorations trying to cope by working extra hours or numbing the pain with alcohol. The world likes to paint Christmas in a positive tone but when we consider why Jesus was born we see an entirely different context.

The savior came to reach a hurting world full of broken people. The reality of Good Friday stands in stark juxtaposition against the image of a newborn baby lying in a manger. He was born to die. His coming was anticipated for thousands of years and was the answer to the timeless question: *Does God care about me?* "The people walking in darkness have seen a great light; on those living in the land of deep darkness a light has dawned."

The Jewish people have a tumultuous history including four hundred years in abject slavery in the land of Egypt. Following that bondage, they were nomadic as they wandered in the Desert of Sinai for forty years. They arrived in the land of promise but wandered away from their God which caused internal strife that divided their nation in two. They were attacked by the Assyrians and Babylonians, deported, and their capitol city razed to the ground multiple times. Centuries would pass as the land would be conquered by the Persians, Greeks, Arabs, Fatimids, Seljuk Turks, Crusaders, Mamelukes, Islamists and others. At the time of the birth of Jesus, the Jews were an occupied people at the hands of the Romans.

The Hebrew prophets had foretold of a savior, the one who would reclaim the throne of David and return the nation to the days of glory. "But you, Bethlehem Ephrathah, though you are small among the clans of Judah, out of you will come for me one who will be ruler over Israel, whose origins are from of old, from ancient times." The people of Israel had spent centuries waiting for things to be different.

> For to us a child is born, to us a son is given, and the government will be on his shoulders. And he will be called Wonderful Counselor, Mighty God, Everlasting Father, Prince of Peace. Of the greatness of his government and peace there

> will be no end. He will reign on David's throne and over his kingdom, establishing and upholding it with justice and righteousness from that time on and forever. The zeal of the Lord Almighty will accomplish this.
>
> — Isaiah 9:6-7 NIV

During this month-long journey, we will take some time to think about Christmas. We will make stops at each of the traditional parts of the story that are depicted in many of the nativity scenes that decorate our homes. But as we dig below the surface, we will find people struggling with the journey of life. Even on that first Christmas there was heart ache and pain.

The story of Christmas is one of hope. A suffering world in need of a savior is rejoicing at the birth of a baby. All the adult problems fade away as we gaze at the innocence with childlike faith. Whether you are reading this book during the Advent season or at some other point in the calendar year, I hope these reflections find room in your heart. From the simplicity of the shepherds to the majesty of the angels, will your Christmas but focused on spreading the good news? Like Joseph and Mary, you don't have to have all the answers for life's most difficult questions, you only need to be open to the Lord's plan for your life. May you treasure up these things and ponder them in your heart.

---

1. The authors

> Many have undertaken to draw up an account of the things that have been fulfilled among us, just as they were handed down to us by those who from the first were eyewitnesses and servants of the word. With this in mind, since I myself have carefully investigated everything from the beginning, I too decided to write an orderly account for you, most excellent Theophilus, so that you may know the certainty of the things you have been taught.
>
> — Luke 1:1–4 NIV

The details of the life and ministry of Jesus are given in the accounts contained in the four Gospels. The modern believer's gratitude for these books should dramatically increase when we consider the time and effort written communication required at that point in history. Everything took a great amount of energy. Travel was arduous and physical danger was lurking at every step along the way as the disciples sacrificed their very lives to spread the good news to the world. As the generation of disciples that were eyewitnesses to the life of Jesus aged and began to perish, the need for written documentation was accentuated.

Tradition ascribes these books to four men—Matthew, Mark, Luke and John—though some scholars have called that authorship into question. Mark's Gospel was almost certainly the first to be written and was likely a source for the other three, but it contains no record of the birth of Jesus. John's Gospel is generally assumed to be the last one recorded by an aging apostle near the end of his life and he also omits the first thirty years of Jesus's life. Only Matthew and Luke give us details regarding the Christmas story.

Matthew was one of the original twelve Apostles and thus had ample opportunity to learn the nativity stories from Jesus himself. Luke, on the other hand, relied on the accounts of others since he was a disciple of Paul and likely had never met Jesus in person. In both cases, many of the details came from Mary, the only eyewitness that might have been alive when these two gospels were written. One can imagine both Matthew and Luke coming to visit her in her senior years when she was living in the home of the Apostle John long after the crucifixion. But though they each chronicled stories from the same period of time they had a different lens that affected the content they chose to include.

Matthew was born a Jew but had chosen to collect taxes on behalf of the Roman occupation. That decision would have made him very wealthy but cost him the relationships of his family. The Romans needed huge sums of money to fund their vast empire and relied on local people to collect taxes. The tax collectors would pay Rome a fixed amount and were free to exact excess funds and keep them as profit. For that reason, they were notoriously dishonest and the chief of sinners in the eyes of the Jewish people. If Matthew had been disowned by his father, what was going through his mind when Jesus told the parable of the Prodigal Son? The fact that Matthew skips that story in his gospel hints that he did not reconcile with his family.

Perhaps that also explains why Matthew is sometimes described by a different name. In the Gospels of Mark and Luke a publican named Levi leaves his profession and begins to follow Jesus. But Matthew uses the identical story to describe his own calling. Did Matthew give up his birth name of Levi when he was disowned by his family or are the writers referring to two different men? Another interesting detail is that Mark says that Levi was the son of Alphaeus, the same name given for the father of the

Apostle James the Younger. Was the name Alphaeus simple a common name or was there a family relationship between them? If they were brothers that begs the question on why that detail is never mentioned. Unfortunately we are left to only speculate. But we must remember that the authors of the gospels were also broken people with issues of their own.

Luke was a physician by trade with a predisposition for historical accuracy. He is the author of the Book of Acts which chronicles the life of the early church and provides written documentation for the legal defense for his mentor Paul the Apostle. Luke goes out of his way to mention the government leaders as key facts in the context around the life of Jesus. He had traveled with Paul on various missionary journeys and proclaimed the gospel as fact. He was a man of science and approached his writing with the same meticulous precision as his medical profession.

Luke was Greek by birth and wrote his gospel to that audience. He alone gives us the backstory of Elizabeth, Zechariah and the birth of John the Baptist. He was a student of the scripture and felt it was important to explain how Messianic prophecies could be fulfilled regarding both Bethlehem and Nazareth. He describes the dedication in Jerusalem and the prophecies spoken over Jesus. Luke also provides us with the majority of the nativity cast with stories of angels, shepherds and the manger.

But the story of the star, the magi and the flight to Egypt to escape from Herod is provided by Matthew alone. In fact, Matthew even provides a complete genealogical record of Jesus's lineage. Family was important to Matthew, even if his was less than perfect. Matthew could relate to the giving of gifts by the magi because he himself had given up his own treasure.

Those are the men that penned the words that provide the backdrop for the Christmas story. But like all narratives, we are prone to omit and overlook the details that don't fit into the mold that we have created. Christmas is supposed to be happy and filled with joy. The perfect baby sleeping peacefully in the iconic manger as Mary sits reflective and glowing. Joseph the handsome father standing as protector, strong and rugged. Cute little lambs straining for a glimpse of the newborn as majestic monarchs pay homage to the King of Kings with angels singing refrains from Handel's Messiah. Those details make for pretty greeting cards but none of it happened that way.

A teenage pregnancy that threatens to end a young girl's marriage and life. A couple ostracized from their community and forced to undertake a dangerous journey far from the judgmental eyes of their neighbors. A birth among the filth of barnyard animals with no privacy or medical attention. A new mother entertaining strangers while she is still bleeding and racked with pain. An aging father with lingering doubts and fears regarding their future fleeing in the middle of the night just hours ahead of government sanctioned infanticide.

In the weeks to come we will take a journey together through the entire Christmas story pausing just long enough to recognize ourselves along the way. We will examine the hidden truths and expose the common misconceptions regarding the events surrounding the birth of Jesus Christ. We will investigate each of the figurines that we find in the typical nativity scene and determine their historical legitimacy for remaining in our displays. But don't worry, this will not be an exercise in cancel culture unless we mean getting rid of the things that were never meant to be there in the first place.

Jesus is God's gift to a hurting world in desperate need of a savior. Your life is not dirtier than the manger. Your family gatherings do not contain more drama than what happened in Bethlehem. And if you are overwhelmed with anxiety and stress then it might comfort you that Jesus was born in the middle of chaos and uncertainty. The first Christmas was messy but God was in control.

The Spirit of the Sovereign Lord is on me because the Lord has anointed me to proclaim good news to the poor. He has sent me to bind up the brokenhearted, to proclaim freedom for the captives and release from darkness for the prisoners.

—Isa 61:1 NIV

ABOUT THE AUTHOR

J.W. Clark is a licensed minister with Elim Fellowship in Lima, NY. He completed his coursework in missions and cultural studies at Elim Bible Institute. He served as a full-time missionary and assistant pastor in the Republic of Ireland. He is on the teaching team at Legacy Church in Farmington, CT and has spoken in numerous nations across four continents on issues of faith and business. He is an author of thriller novels and Christian nonfiction.

ALSO BY J. W. CLARK

Other Titles in the Think About Series:

Book 1: Think About the Kingdom

Book 2: Think About Your Response

Book 3: Think About Christmas

NOTES

1. Worry (Matt 6:25–34)

1. https://www.washingtonpost.com/outlook/five-myths/five-myths-about-the-lottery/2019/12/27/742b9662-2664-11ea-ad73-2fd294520e97_story.html
2. Matthew 6:25, 27 ESV
3. https://www.yourhormones.info/hormones/adrenaline
4. Matt 6:30
5. Matt 6:34 NIV

2. Everyone Needs a Cause (Acts 6–9)

1. Acts 6:8
2. Acts 7:54 NIV
3. Acts 7:60 NIV
4. Acts 8:39
5. Acts 9:4 NIV
6. Acts 9:15 NIV

3. The Enemy of My Enemy Is Not My Friend (Matt 26:14–27:10)

1. John 12:3
2. John 11:33–34
3. John 12:6
4. https://study.com/academy/lesson/dantes-inferno-canto-34-summary-quotes.html
5. Matt 27:3
6. 2 Cor 10:4
7. 2 Cor 11:14

8. Rom 2:4
9. John 21:15-22
10. Song 2:15

4. Passion for the Wrong Cause (John 18:1–11)

1. John 11:8
2. John 11:16 NIV
3. John 2:13–17
4. Ps 69:9 NIV
5. Matt 11:12 ESV
6. Matt 26:53 ESV
7. Luke 22:51
8. John 18:10
9. https://www.christianstudylibrary.org/article/healing-malchus%E2%80%99s-ear
10. John 18:15–18, 25–27
11. John 21:15

5. Distracted Passion (Luke 10:38–42)

1. Matt 6:24
2. 1 Pet 4:9
3. Luke 10:40 NIV
4. John 12:3,7
5. Matt 9:37 NIV

6. Don't Assume God Is on Your Side (Josh 5:13–6:27)

1. Josh 5:13
2. Josh 5:15 GNT

3. https://bible.org/article/captain-lord%E2%80%99s-army-joshua-513-15
4. https://www.christianity.com/wiki/bible/what-is-the-biblical-significance-of-the-number-7.html
5. Deut 15:1–2
6. https://www.christianity.com/wiki/bible/what-is-the-biblical-significance-of-the-number-7.html
7. Rev 1:4
8. Judg 1:2
9. Gen 29:35
10. Heb 13:2
11. Jer 29:11

7. Fake News (John 8)

1. Lev 20:10
2. Matt 5:17
3. John 8:10-11 NIV

8. Armed for Battle (Eph 6:10–20)

1. https://www.history.com/shows/hatfields-and-mccoys/articles/the-hatfield-mccoy-feud
2. https://www.cbsnews.com/news/official-end-of-legendary-feud
3. 2 Cor 11:23–27
4. https://www.ziglar.com/quotes/when-you-throw-dirt-at-people/

9. Hate For Those Who Hate (Luke 9:51–56)

1. https://www.bibleodyssey.org/en/people/related-articles/samaritans
2. Luke 9:54 NIV

3. https://www.history.com/topics/19th-century/labor

10. Respond, Don't React (Acts 15:36–16:24)

1. Acts 16:17 ESV
2. 2 Tim 4:11 NIV
3. https://www.newadvent.org/fathers/0817.htm

11. God Cares about the Little Things (John 2:1–11)

1. https://www.focusonthefamily.ca/content/why-is-there-no-marriage-in-heaven
2. Eph 3:20
3. Luke 6:38 NIV
4. https://www.biblestudy.org/bibleref/meaning-of-numbers-in-bible/6.html
5. John 19:30
6. https://www.oaoa.com/people/religion/apostle-john-jesus-s-closest-friend/article_66aeb1c8-e337-11ea-a79c-1b6e634db0de.html
7. https://bible.org/article/historical-reliability-gospels
8. Heb 4:16 ESV
9. John 2:5 NIV

12. It May Look Like I'm Surrounded - (2 Kgs 6:8–23)

1. https://www.scientificamerican.com/article/how-fast-is-the-earth-mov
2. 2 Kgs 6:15 NIV
3. 2 Kgs 6:16 NIV
4. 2 Kgs 2:11

5. 2 Cor 10:4 ESV

13. Family Drama (Gen 25–33)

1. Gen 25:33
2. Gen 27:41 ESV
3. Gen 31:9
4. Gen 31:19
5. Gen 31:3 NIV

14. Guarded Treasure (2 Kgs 18–20)

1. 2 Kings 16:3
2. Numbers 21:9
3. John 3:14
4. https://ericpeoples.co
5. 2 Kgs 18:29, 31 ESV
6. 2 Kgs 20:17–18 NIV
7. 2 Chr 32:31
8. https://www.bible-history.com/map_babylonian_captivity/map_of_the_deportation_of_judah_the_destruction_of_jerusalem.html

15. The Fire of Conviction (Daniel 1–3)

1. 2 Kgs 20:17
2. 2 Kgs 25:1
3. 2 Kgs 20:18
4. Dan 3:15 NIV
5. Dan 4:19
6. Heb 11:1
7. Michael Youssef, https://www.ltw.org
8. 2 Cor 2:15 NIV
9. Dan 3:28 NIV

16. Drowning in Noise (Matt 14:22–34)

1. Matt 14:27 CEB
2. Matt 14:31 NASB

17. Do You Want to Get Well? (John 5:1–15)

1. John 5:6 NIV
2. John 5:7 NIV
3. John 5:7 NIV

18. How Did I End Up Here? (1 Kgs 19:1–18)

1. 1 Kgs 19:2 NIV
2. http://www.jewishencyclopedia.com/articles/13766-sinai-mount
3. Exod 3:1
4. Exod 33:6
5. Exod 34:1
6. Exod 17:6
7. Deut 1:6
8. Exod 33:19
9. 1 Kgs 19:9
10. 1 Kgs 19:10 NIV
11. 1 Kgs 19:13 NIV
12. Jer 29:11 NIV
13. 1 Kgs 19:15 NIV
14. Deut 1:6
15. Ps 139:16 NIV
16. Isa 46:10

19. Ministers of Reconciliation (2 Cor 5:14–21)

1. https://www.biblica.com/resources/scholar-notes/niv-study-bible/intro-to-2-corinthians/
2. 2 Cor 5:19–20 NIV
3. 2 Cor 5:17
4. Luke 23:34 CEV

20. Who Is My Neighbor? (Luke 10:25–37)

1. Luke 10:25 NIV
2. Luke 10:26 GNT
3. Luke 10:29 NIV
4. Ex 20:17
5. https://www.medindia.net/patients/calculators/world-death-clock.asp
6. https://bible.org/illustration/hatred-between-jews-and-samaritans

21. Undebatable Truth (Acts 15)

1. Acts 13:47 NIV
2. https://www.openbible.info/blog/2012/07/calculating-the-time-and-cost-of-pauls-missionary-journeys/
3. http://jewishencyclopedia.com/articles/4391-circumcision#2
4. Prov 11:14, 12:15, 15:22
5. Acts 10–11
6. Acts 10:47

22. Words Matter (Luke 7:18–35)

1. Mark 9:23 NIV
2. Luke 8:29 ESV
3. Matt 12:24
4. Jas 3:6
5. Prov 18:21

23. The Gospel Truth (Luke 4:14–30)

1. Luke 4:1
2. Isa 61:2 NIV
3. Isa 61:3
4. Isa 61:4–9
5. Luke 4:21 NIV

24. Send Someone Else (Exodus 2–4)

1. Hab 2:3 NLT
2. Rom 11:29
3. Exodus 3:6 NIV
4. Exodus 4:10 NIV
5. Ex 4:13 CEV
6. Matt 9:37 NIV

25. The Opportunity to Complain (Mark 6:30–44)

1. Mark 6:31 NIV
2. Mark 6:35 NLT
3. Mark 6:37 NIV
4. John 12:6
5. John 6:9
6. Mark 8:1–13

26. Who Do You Think You Are? (John 8:12–59)

1. John 1:9–11
2. https://www.dictionary.com/browse/confirmation-bias
3. John 8:39 NIV
4. John 8:48
5. John 8:53 NIV
6. John 8:58 NIV

27. Infinite Blessings (Luke 15:11–32)

1. Deut 21:17
2. Num 27:4
3. Ruth 4:1–4
4. Luke 15:11 NIV
5. https://ericpeoples.co/
6. https://www.investopedia.com/terms/z/zero-sumgame.asp
7. Matt 14:22–36; Mark 6:45–56; John 6:16–24
8. Matt 17:27

28. Don't Blame Me (Genesis 3)

1. Gen 3:3 NIV, emphasis added
2. Gen 3:9 NIV
3. https://www.merriam-webster.com/words-at-play/gate-suffix-scandal-word-history
4. https://behumanproject.org/why-are-we-tribal/
5. Matt 7:3–5
6. Prov 18:21, Jas 3:3–6, Matt 12:36, et al
7. Jas 2:14–17

29. Dry Bones (Ezekiel 37)

1. Ps 23:3 NKJV
2. Rom 4:17 ESV
3. Ezek 37:3 NIV
4. Ps 36:9
5. Isa 46:10
6. Ezek 22:30
7. Gen 1:2
8. 1 Kgs 17:17–24
9. Mark 8:22–25
10. Ezek 37:11 CEB
11. Exod 34:29
12. Matt 17:4

30. What Do You Have Left? (Mark 12:41–44, Luke 21:1–4)

1. https://nonprofitssource.com/online-giving-statistics/church-giving
2. Matt 6:21 NIV
3. https://churchleaders.com/outreach-missions/outreach-missions-articles/314227-2350-bible-verses-money.html
4. John 2:15
5. https://www.investopedia.com/articles/personal-finance/050615/are-you-top-one-percent-world.asp
6. https://fortune.com/2015/09/30/america-wealth-inequality/
7. https://www.pewsocialtrends.org/2020/01/09/trends-in-income-and-wealth-inequality/
8. https://givingpledge.org/
9. https://www.charitychoices.com/page/how-much-given-whom-what

31. Count Me In (2 Sam 24)

1. 1 Sam 17:34–36
2. 1 Sam 13:14
3. 2 Sam 24:14 NIV
4. 1 Sam 16:11, 17:28
5. Absalom in 2 Sam 15, Adonijah in 1 Kgs 1
6. Amnon in 2 Sam 13
7. Absalom in 2 Sam 13:28–29
8. Jonathan, son of Saul in 1 Sam 31:2
9. Bathsheba and Uriah in 2 Sam 11
10. 2 Sam 24:24 ESV

www.ingramcontent.com/pod-product-compliance
Lightning Source LLC
Chambersburg PA
CBHW071959040426
42447CB00009B/1400

* 9 7 8 1 7 3 5 7 5 9 3 4 0 *